In the
SHADOW
of GRACE

D1602264

In the
SHADOW
of GRACE

The Life and Meditations of
G. CAMPBELL MORGAN

COMPILED AND EDITED BY
RICHARD, HOWARD,
AND JOHN MORGAN

BakerBooks
Grand Rapids, Michigan

Published by Baker Books
a division of Baker Publishing Group
P.O. Box 6287, Grand Rapids, MI 49516-6287
www.bakerbooks.com

Printed in the United States of America

Library of Congress Cataloging-in-Publication Data
In the shadow of grace : the life and meditations of G. Campbell Morgan / compiled
and edited by Richard, Howard, and John Morgan.
   p. cm.
   Includes bibliographical references.
   ISBN 10: 0-8010-6817-7 (pbk.)
   ISBN 978-0-8010-6817-1 (pbk.)
   1. Morgan, G. Campbell (George Campbell), 1863–1945. 2. Consola-
tion. I. Morgan, Richard Lyon, 1929– II. Morgan, Howard, 1941–
III. Morgan, John, 1935– IV. Morgan, G. Campbell (George Campbell),
1863–1945. Selections. 2007.
  BX7260.M555I67 2007
  242′.4—dc22   2007002632

In keeping with biblical principles of
creation stewardship, Baker Publishing Group advocates the responsible
use of our natural resources. As a
member of the Green Press Initiative,
our company uses recycled paper
when possible. The text paper of
this book is comprised of 30% post-
consumer waste.

It is a great thing to find that, even though vigor decreases, the light on the road abides, and though earthly shadows may be lengthening, one does not feel one is going down the hill, but up.

G. Campbell Morgan

In memory of our grandfather,
G. Campbell Morgan,
Bible teacher and preacher

The journey long, the time soon gone:
    Sail on. Sail on.
The sea is deep, your promise keep:
    Sail on. Sail on.
Though ocean wide, no surging tide:
    Sail on, sail on.
Home, home at last, the storm is past.
    Sail on, sail on.

Contents

Foreword   9
Introduction   15

1. Eclipse of Faith and Transformation of Life   23
2. Rejected on Earth, Accepted in Heaven   33
3. When Loved Ones Die   43
4. Confronting Illness   53
5. When Tragedy Strikes   65
6. Dreams Deferred   81
7. Growing Older   93
8. Facing the End of Life   101

Conclusion: Transformed by Grace   111
Suggested Readings   123
Notes   127
List of Biblical Texts   135
List of Sermon Titles   137

Foreword

I realize today that the ten years of Bible teaching have produced results which cannot be tabulated, and which are far
in excess of anything I could have imagined. . . . Students
here have passed through our Friday classes and have gone
here and there and everywhere in this land and to the ends
of the earth.

G. Campbell Morgan

The power of teaching combined with the power of the
Word—these together have the potential for truly exponential
influence, especially as exercised by G. Campbell Morgan. I
think, however, that Campbell Morgan might be surprised
that even in the first decade of a new millennium there are
results of his work that will need to be added to the final
tabulation. G. Campbell Morgan is teaching today at Chicago
Theological Seminary (CTS).

The only seminary degree Campbell Morgan received
was from the Chicago Theological Seminary in 1902. Yet
his enormous output and influential preaching was virtu-
ally unknown at the seminary in the late twentieth century

when a new member joined the board of trustees of CTS. Howard Morgan, grandson of G. Campbell Morgan, was recruited for the seminary's board as he transitioned out of a successful career in banking into increased volunteer work. Howard Morgan also began, in this period, to catalogue his grandfather's papers. He was surprised, to say the least, when he discovered that the seminary whose board he had just joined was the one from which his grandfather held his only seminary degree. Howard Morgan found and framed the graduation hood from that 1902 ceremony. This hood now hangs on the seminary's wall.

It seemed fitting, therefore, when Howard Morgan was elected to chair the Chicago Theological Seminary board of trustees in 2000, that his installation ceremony include a sermon of his grandfather's. Dean Dow Edgerton, whose field is homiletics, was pleased to be asked to wade into the mighty corpus of the G. Campbell Morgan preaching output, and he selected "Suffer the Little Children." Dean Edgerton writes,

> Reading the sermons of others is a regular part of a preacher's work, but actually preaching someone else's words is a different matter. Morgan's preaching context required a much more expansive treatment than we commonly undertake now, and his expository style gave ample scope for exploring the internal logic of the Scripture and the contemporary moment in which he preached. He moved effortlessly (an "effortlessness" that requires great effort, in fact) between the text and the time and the business of bills pending before the Houses of Parliament. How to reduce a forty-five minute sermon, and one of such thoughtful, intricate, and creative composition, to the twenty minutes allowed in a chapel service? I decided to focus on the parts that communicated his distinctive passion of mind, spirit, and heart. Here is what I discovered: saying his words in my voice let me hear a new possibility for my own voice, and to imagine a passion bequeathed by blessed elder that could in fact become my own.[1]

In hearing this sermon preached by Dean Edgerton, the entire community of CTS was struck by how much G. Campbell Morgan embodied the seminary's current vision statement. His depth of encounter with the Scriptures combined with an informed and specific message of social justice resonated strongly with our institutional pledge to produce religious leaders who can "transform the world toward greater justice and mercy." Campbell Morgan was recognized as one of our own. It was also of great interest to the students that there were many, many other such sermons now to be found in the library. And for hardworking students who also serve churches, a deep well of good preaching that they can draw from when the need is acute was good news indeed. The Morgan library continues to be popular, especially around exam time.

In addition to this service to students, for the last four years the Morgan family has also given a cash prize for a seminary student competition in expository preaching in the G. Campbell Morgan style. A selection committee reads the submissions and nominates a winner. The winner then preaches the G. Campbell Morgan sermon at the seminary's alumni days, Ministerial Institute. Three of the four winners of the G. Campbell Morgan Preaching Prize have been African-American, two of them women.[2] It is unsurprising, when one considers what tradition today best embodies profound spirituality, tremendous love of the Scriptures, and a sense of the *times*, that those who carry on the tradition of expository preaching are of the African-American tradition. But it is also interesting that it is the women's preaching that captures so well the spirit of G. Campbell Morgan in paying very close attention to the world. I was reminded of the reflection of an African-American woman religious leader who is a character in Toni Morrison's work *Paradise*. This character reflects, "Playing blind was to avoid the language God spoke in. He did not thunder instructions or whisper messages into ears. Oh, no. He was a liberating God: A teacher who taught you how to learn, to see for yourself. His signs were clear, abundantly so, if you stopped steeping in vanity's soul juice and paid attention to His world."[3] For Campbell Morgan, God is a teacher who taught him how to see if he (and others) "stopped steeping in vanity's soul" and paid attention.

Another startling aspect of Campbell Morgan's work and influence today is the timeliness of the message. My favorite Campbell Morgan sermon is the one that followed the sinking of the *Titanic*. In that sermon this great theologian avoids the Scylla of a puppeteer version of divine providence and the Charybdis of a humanity alone and adrift in a purposeless sea of historical events. "Those of us who are Christian men and women need to be careful about what we say about this catastrophe. . . . This is not a divine judgment. We are face to face with the infinite mystery of the meaning and method of the Divine Government. . . . To speak of this catastrophe as a judgment of God is to entirely deny the biblical doctrine of God. The iceberg was the act of God; the *Titanic* was the act of man." Terrorist attacks, tsunamis, hurricanes, genocide, and war characterize our time in this twenty-first century. "Where is God?" is an important question to ask, but it is supremely important, following G. Campbell Morgan's lead, to take extreme care in how we answer that question. Much of public religious rhetoric on the momentous events of the twenty-first century, by contrast to Campbell Morgan, is not so careful. In fact, one might go so far as to say it is careless.

On a personal note, I must say I was cheered to find out that G. Campbell Morgan had been a seminary president. And he, like I, found it difficult but rewarding work. I often wish I could consult him on a number of items regarding the difficulties of leading these peculiar institutions, peculiar because they are children of both higher education and the churches. Here again I expect I would receive great wisdom.

The preparation of women and men for ministry at Chicago Theological Seminary has been greatly aided by the teaching of G. Campbell Morgan. I hope he believes his seminary has been a credit to him.

Rev. Dr. Susan Brooks Thistlethwaite,
president and professor of theology,
Chicago Theological Seminary

Introduction

After hearing many family stories about our illustrious grandfather, G. Campbell Morgan, named one of the ten greatest Christian preachers of the twentieth century by the contributing board of *Preaching* magazine, it was easy to put him on a pedestal. The editors listed him sixth among the top ten, immediately behind Martin Luther King Jr. and Harry Emerson Fosdick. They wrote of him: "Called by many 'the prince of expositors,' G. Campbell Morgan helped influence the shape of evangelical preaching on both sides of the Atlantic. Born in England, raised in Wales, Morgan lacked formal education, but his absolute confidence in Scripture made him an avid student and interpreter of the Word."[1]

Growing up in the parsonage of a Philadelphia Presbyterian church served at different times both by our grandfather and our father, we could not escape our grandfather's powerful and sometimes intimidating presence. After all, he was someone whose evangelical preaching reached masses of people on both sides of the Atlantic. It made it difficult for our father, his son, to live up to his father's acclaim, doubly so because he learned to preach under Campbell Morgan's mentorship. In the shadow of a clerical giant, others may find it difficult to find their place in the sun. For us, Campbell Morgan was part myth and part grandfather, and when we were children, the myths were strong.

One of us (Richard) recalls Campbell Morgan's last visit to the United States in 1937. "I vividly remember visiting him in a hotel, and he was working a crossword puzzle. I also remember being impressed by the huge crowd that came to hear him preach his last sermon there, and loudspeakers being set up in the downstairs hall. I have no idea what he said, I only recall a lean, white-haired gentleman who had a great voice. Dad let me go with Campbell Morgan and his wife, Annie, to New York City to see them off on the *Queen Mary*. I do remember Campbell Morgan saying to Dad: 'This will be the fifty-fourth and last trip across the Atlantic. We will not set foot on American soil again.' He was seventy-five years old at the time, and two years later World War II broke out."

It was not until the three of us made a 2005 journey to England and Wales to discover where our grandfather was born and the congregations he served that we began to see that while he was a famous preacher, he was also a human being who struggled with some of the same life issues we faced—two of us as ministers ourselves and one as board chair of a theological school, the same one that awarded Campbell Morgan his only advanced seminary degree. In many ways, it was comforting to discover Campbell Morgan as a living, struggling human being, not a myth or a figure on a pedestal. We learned to appreciate his life and faith more because we could feel more deeply the crises he faced. We felt connected to his struggles because we had faced some ourselves, as have most people; and we felt renewed by his faith—wrestled out of life like Jacob wrestling with the divine, guided by the biblical witness, but transformed into words and deeds for others.

Whether traveling to see the modest house in which he was born in 1863 in Tetbury, England; standing in the schoolroom of a Welsh Methodist church where he gave his first sermon at the age of thirteen; visiting towns where he served Congregational churches in Stone, Rugeley, or Birmingham, England; or standing in the Westminster Congregational Church pulpit in London; we began to rediscover G. Campbell Morgan, whose life now took on flesh and bone meaning for us.

It was one day while we were standing near Tintern Abbey in the Wye Valley of Wales, a region where he would take what he called "trundlings" (unhurried visits), that the idea for this book began to take shape. We came to see that with all the volumes he wrote or the books or articles written about him, none had centered on his life crises and the faith that arose out of them. We decided to find a way to let our grandfather speak for himself across the centuries to a new generation of Christians and seekers.

It is true that our grandfather had from time to time inserted references to his own struggles in sermons, but because he focused so lovingly on the biblical text, it often seemed he was apologetic for bringing himself into the mix. In a 1909 sermon, "Jacob's Lameness," he confessed:

> I have known the desperate struggle against God. I have known what it has been to find his hand laid so heavily upon my life that life has become weak, broken, helpless; and I have known what it is like to come to the morning that broke after the darkness, and say: "I have seen God face to face, and my life is healed."[2]

Again, in a sermon entitled "The Crippling That Crowns," Campbell Morgan offered these forthright words:

Inevitably, sooner or later, there comes a crisis . . . in which we are brought to the appalling sense of our own incompetence and weakness. That is a great hour, an hour of overwhelming disappointment merging to despair; the result of which we shall never again be what we were, but we shall go softly all our days.[3]

Preaching from the Westminster Pulpit in 1904, Campbell Morgan meditated on his life, especially God's hand in it: "For God is my witness. He has given me my share of sorrow's sacrament, days of awful heart-break, when all the lights along the shore seem to go out."[4]

We began to feel not only a deeper connection to our grandfather but also a new awareness that his faith was not "cheap grace" (words offered by the martyred German pastor Dietrich Bonhoeffer to describe faith without suffering, without the cross). Campbell Morgan's life crises were not set apart from his faith but rather arose out of the struggles through which he learned to follow Jesus more closely and out of which arose some of the passionate convictions of his sermons. And we realized that his crises were those experienced by most of us if we are honest with ourselves and God.

What were these crises in G. Campbell Morgan's life? There were many, some hidden because they were unspoken, but others discovered as we journeyed with him through our travels and through studies of his sermons and letters, many of them never before published. One of us was the keeper of the Campbell Morgan letters, sermons, and other materials, which provided a window into his life not open to many. Many of these written materials are now stored in the Chicago Theological Seminary library.

Early in his life our grandfather experienced a crisis of faith. He locked up all his books except the Bible, vowing to study it until he either accepted or rejected what he found. He faced rejection in his youth too, once by the Methodists because they felt he never would make a preacher, and again in his first parish ministry. When Campbell Morgan's father heard about his son's rejection by the Methodists, he responded: "Rejected on earth . . . accepted in heaven," words that have come down through our family memories.

Throughout his long life he felt the sting of losses brought about by the deaths of his young sister, daughter, mother and father, and best friend and ministerial colleague, Albert Swift. He dealt with illness and what we today might call "burnout" because his speaking and evangelistic journeys were incredibly taxing. In 1936 he estimated he had preached nearly 24,000 times. He faced national tragedy, two world wars, and the sinking of the *Titanic*. A letter to one of his sons in 1941 describes only one such event that happened in London:

> Yes, we were alright on the night of May 10. We spent the night in the shelter. It was certainly a terrible night, but we were kept safe. Certain incendiary bombs fell on St. Ermin's (St. Ermin's was the hotel he stayed in during the later years of his life and where he died in 1945), but they were promptly dealt with. However, next morning the whole neighborhood was a scene of charred remains.[5]

When he was facing growing old and facing death, life was made more difficult by the simple fact that in spite of all his books and travels, he had little finances left to sustain him during his final years. In a letter to a son who had offered to help him financially, he confessed how wartime and retirement had limited his finances.[6]

But however difficult his struggles, our grandfather seemed to understand how God used even losses to deepen his faith.

In reminiscing about his nearly seventy years on earth, he wrote: "I think the Holy Spirit often does irregular things that are nevertheless regular in the economy of God," calling attention to his times of struggles from health problems, waning strength, and sometimes blocked paths he wanted to follow but later realized were not God's will.[7]

Never suppose you know anyone completely, even a member of your family. In finding crises in our grandfather's life we had not completely known before, we also took comfort and no small measure of hope in understanding how these wounds became sources of his living faith. As he once wrote: "The greatest victory obtainable in this life is that of fulfilling the possibilities of personality, and the greatest defeat is that of failure in this direction. . . . Success consists in living, not in gain; not in the reward of doing, but in the doing."[8]

The title of this book, *In the Shadow of Grace*, was very carefully thought out. Faith is not living in the sunshine all the time, but also learning that life's troubles can be occasions for discovering God's presence—something G. Campbell Morgan learned in a number of difficult times in his life, whether through the loss of a young child or a troubled first ministry. While life's troubles can sometimes make us feel like we are living in shadows, grace reminds us that shadows are not possible without the sun, without the light of grace. In fact, without the sun, shadows become permanent darkness. G. Campbell Morgan knew shadows in his life as each one of us knows the same in ours. Grace is God's promise of light, which is always there even if we are not aware of it. For this reason, the words of the psalmist seem fitting: "He that dwelleth in the secret place of the Most High shall abide under the shadow of the Almighty. . . . Because he has set his love upon me, therefore I will deliver him. With long life I will satisfy him, and show him my salvation" (Ps. 91:14, 16).

This book is our attempt to let G. Campbell Morgan speak out of his own life crises, believing it is precisely at such times that each one of us can connect not only with his struggles but with the deep faith that sustained him. These are words to be studied as he might have studied a biblical text—slowly, reading the words many times through, letting them reach you as his spoken words reached thousands.

We are grateful to our family in the United States and England for their support, and to many others we encountered as we traveled, especially the ministers of congregations he served in London and Birmingham, UK, and the librarian of the seminary he once served as president of Cheshunt College, Cambridge University.

We debated whether to change various passages that are not gender inclusive (he used the word *man* rather than *person*, for example) but decided to leave the words as he wrote or spoke them, while we also note that very early in his ministry he advocated for the larger role of women in the life of the church, indeed fostering their involvement in his own ministries, most especially at Westminster Congregational Church in London.

It is our hope that this volume will inspire readers to read his other books (a list of a few selected books by G. Campbell Morgan or about him are provided at the end of this book). In addition to reissuing his ten-volume *Westminster Pulpit*, three other books of his have been reissued and other new volumes are now being considered.

We are especially indebted to Chicago Theological Seminary for its willingness to house the G. Campbell Morgan library and lend their support to our efforts as members of the Morgan Family Trust.

Richard Lyon Morgan,
Howard Campbell Morgan,
John Crossley Morgan

G. Campbell when he began his ministry
at Westminster Chapel, 1904.

1 Eclipse of Faith and Transformation of Life

In the course of preparation for teaching at the age of sixteen, Campbell Morgan found himself confronted with the rationalistic and materialistic philosophies of the late nineteenth century. Morgan felt he could not know religious truths with certitude, and he found his belief in the authority of the Bible challenged, with no substitute for his childhood faith. He called this experience an "eclipse of faith": "I was as honest then, as now," he wrote in his diary. "And gradually faith, while not undermined, was eclipsed. When the sun is eclipsed, the light is not killed, it is hidden. There came a moment when I was sure of nothing." [1]

The Bible, which had been the bedrock of the faith Morgan learned from his father, George Morgan, no longer had authority. In his despair, he took all his books and locked them in a cupboard. Years later, he commented he could still hear the click of the key. He went to a bookshop and bought a new Bible. He wrote, "If it is the Word of God, and I come to it with an unprejudiced and open mind, it will bring assurance of itself. The Bible *found* me." [2]

This young, aspiring teacher's life was transformed by the rediscovery of biblical truths. From that moment in 1883, he became "A man of the Word." In his later sermons, Campbell Morgan was always compassionate toward doubters, and he claimed only people of faith had doubts. In many of his writings and sermons, Morgan attested to his transformation through the Bible. He exemplified the Benedictine tradition of *lectio divina*, reading the Bible not for information but transformation. During an address delivered in 1901 in Northfield, Massachusetts, he warned of the dangers of an intellectual approach to the Bible and of a dishonest use of biblical texts to justify preconceived beliefs. In a real sense, Morgan understood the danger of reading the Bible to be compatible with theologies and beliefs without letting the Bible speak for itself. In a sermon preached at Westminster Congregational Church, London, he spoke of how the Bible came alive for him.

The other disciples therefore said unto him, We have seen the Lord. But he [Thomas] said unto them, Except I shall see in his hands the print of the nails, and put my finger into his side, I will not believe.

John 20:25

Firm foothold for faith has often to be found by fighting, and let no man who has ever had to enter into that conflict be angry with the man who has . . . do not criticize the man who is fighting, the man who has to face the spectres of the mind.[3]

The popular epithet applied to Thomas is that of the doubter . . . "Except I shall see . . . I will not believe." It was the language of absolute honesty, the language of a man who would not be credulous. He declined to profess a faith he did not possess.[4]

[Thomas] was a man at once cautious and courageous. . . . We speak of Thomas as a skeptic. . . . He was a skeptic. He was a man who was compelled to investigate, to inquire . . . a man who would make no confession of faith, of hope, of confidence unless it was a confession absolutely honest, true to the profoundest convictions of the mind.[5]

Again, let the man whose faith is assailed deal directly, immediately with Christ. This man Thomas dealt directly with the Lord, and it was thus that he came to victory. . . .

Turn from all human interpretations, turn from all theological systems, from all preachers and teachers, as well as priests, and turn to the Christ of the New Testament. Do it honestly. Gather up all your books about Christ, whether by believers or unbelievers, and lock them up and fling away the key. Take the New Testament . . . I do not believe that any man here will take the New Testament stories, steeping his soul in them, making himself acquainted with the Man presented there; but that the issue of it sooner or later must be that he will come to say what Thomas said, "My Lord and my God."[6]

I would utter a paradox; it is only the man of faith who really doubts; there is no room for doubt unless you believe in God.[7]

The very last word I utter is to the man in doubt. Find your way to Christ for yourself, not to the Christ of the preacher, or of the schoolmen, or of ecclesiastical systems, or the Christ of the whole Church, but the Christ of the New Testament. Tell Him all your doubts, and griefs, and fears, and you will know He is the living One speaking through His Word as surely as He spoke directly to Thomas and in Him alone, you will find the rest for which you are seeking.[8]

> They said to each other, "Were not our hearts burning within us while he talked to us on the road, while he was opening the scriptures to us?"
>
> Luke 24:32 RSV

Have you ever felt as I have, that you would have given almost everything to have heard Him interpret the Scriptures? They did not know the Man talking to them was the One of whom He was talking. They did see a new meaning in their own Scriptures. . . . There broke upon them a new vision of the truth, a new understanding of the things with which they were perfectly familiar, and in this new vision they found new understanding of all the things which they had long known.[9]

The only way in which it is possible to "feed on Christ" is through the Word of God. Simply to study the Bible from an intellectual standpoint in order to know it, is not to feed on Him and, moreover, such study is not sufficient.[10]

We had better never handle the Bible than learn it by letter without being obedient to its call and claim so that our lives may be *transformed* by its message.[11]

In the Scriptures, those self-same Scriptures through which He spake to men of old, listen for them. The study of the Bible will curse us in the next ten years if we are not careful. Men will tabulate and analyze and think they know everything. . . . Listen, unless as a result of your study of the Bible you hear the imperial tone, *the voice of the living Christ talking in your inmost soul,* your Bible knowledge is a mere technique that will burn and ruin you. . . . No man or woman, young man or young woman, youth or maiden, will cultivate the habit of waiting to listen for the direct message of Christ and be disappointed. Then your Bible will be a new book.[12]

> You search the scriptures, because you think that in them you have eternal life; and it is they that bear witness to me; yet you refuse to come to me that you may have life.
>
> John 5:39 RSV

I am profoundly grateful for the new interest being manifested everywhere in the Scriptures of truth, but one cannot help being afraid lest in the midst of this very interest there should be failure. We need most carefully to ponder these words of Jesus which were addressed to people who were familiar with and earnest students of the Scriptures. . . . Unless we are very careful we may be urgent and earnest in our study of the Scriptures, and yet fail as disastrously as did the men of Christ's own time. The fact that a man knows the Books does not mean that he knows Christ.[13]

The other peril that threatens us is that of dishonesty. . . . How can we be dishonest with Scripture? A man is always in danger of being dishonest with Scripture when he comes to it with preconceived notions of any sort. There is no more perilous method than that of coming to the Bible in order to prove from it something you have already made up your mind to.[14]

You are seeking life, but you are making the mistake of imagining that in the actual words of Scripture there is the mystic life, which becomes yours simply because you know them. . . . They accepted of their own Scriptures only those which appealed to their prejudices and desires. They denied or rejected all the rest.[15]

In the name of God I beseech you to come to the study of this Book . . . by searching the Scripture, by finding your way to Him, who is the ultimate. That is the meaning of the words we sing, "Beyond the sacred page, I seek Thee, Lord." May God help us to do it in the days that are to come.[16]

The Bible is a spiritual book. It will never satisfy you if you merely come to it from the literary standpoint, to find out scientific facts. But if you come to it and read its treatment of all these in the light of the invisible and spiritual, it will more than satisfy you. . . . Through all life, in its early morning, and in that hot mid-day when the battle thickens, and in that golden light of evening, you will always find the very word you want, the very strength and help you need.[17]

A hundred years later these words of G. Campbell Morgan are prophetic of a "famine for the Word of God" in our time. Biblical illiteracy remains rampant in most mainline churches, and careful study and meditation of the Word of God is scarce.

> Behold, the days come, saith the Lord Jehovah, that I will send a famine in the land, not a famine of bread, nor a thirst for water, but of hearing the words of Jehovah.
>
> Amos 8:11

First of all, this famine of lack of the Word of God . . . Not that God ceases to speak, but that man loses his power to hear. Not that God withholds His Word from men, but

that men hear it, and never hear it. . . . I am sometimes told
that the Word of God has been sadly neglected for many
years—and alas, I am sure it is true; but it declared that the
reason is that men outside the Church and within the Church
have been indulging in what we speak of as Criticism, Higher
and Lower. Nothing of the kind. The thing that has sealed
the Word of God to the believer is the believer's unbelief
and disobedience and idolatry. It is our own idolatry that
robs us of the consciousness of the living sustenance of the
Word of God.[18]

The word of the Lord abideth for ever.

1 Peter 1:25

On one of the highways near the heart of London's city
stand two great publishing houses. The one is of that of the
Times newspaper, and the other is that of the British and
Foreign Bible Society. Over the first is a clock and figure of
Father Time, suggestive of things transient and passing. On
the façade of the other is an open Bible with the words of
my text inscribed thereon: "The Word of the Lord endureth
forever;" a reminder, in the midst of transient and passing and
perishing things, of the things that abide. . . . The Church
without the Word is a lamp without a light. She may be well
organised, ornate and beautiful in her ritual, influential in her
worldly possessions, intellectual grasp upon certain truths; but
save as she is proclaiming the Word of the Lord that endureth
for ever in the midst of the age that passes and perishes, she
is a lampstand without a light. Therefore the abiding need
of the Church is a knowledge of the Word of God, and an
obedience to the Word of God.[19]

Campbell Morgan was asked the question in 1825, "Is doubt sinful?" This letter was his answer.

Doubts are by no means sinful. The limitations of our finite minds must create problems for us at times. You get a perfect illustration of this in the prophecy of Habakkuk. In it you find a revelation of how to deal with them. He declared them to God, which proved his faith and gave God the opportunity to answer him.[20]

Campbell Morgan teaching Bible at Friday night services
at Westminster Chapel. Date unknown, circa 1909–13.

G. Campbell Morgan in the pulpit at Westminster Chapel, 1910.

2 Rejected on Earth, Accepted in Heaven

On May 2, 1888, Campbell Morgan stood in the Lichfield Road Church pulpit in Birmingham, England, to give a sermon that he hoped would gain him entrance to the Wesleyan Methodist ministry. He was accustomed to larger audiences than the some seventy-five persons who had gathered to judge his sermon. He made a practice later to look out over those gathered to hear him so he could prepare himself ahead of time. In London's Westminster Church, one can still find a small peephole in a wall where Morgan could look out before he entered the sanctuary to preach.

Two weeks after giving the trial sermon, Campbell Morgan received notice that he had been rejected. He was devastated at first and wrote in his journal, "Very dark. Everything seems still. He knoweth best." He wired his father a one-word message: "Rejected." His father's wired reply was swift: "Rejected on earth. Accepted in heaven."[1]

Rejection in any form is emotionally traumatic, sometimes shaking the very foundations of a person's life, leaving self-doubts and recriminations. It must have been very difficult for a young man who felt called to ministry to have been told that his sermon was not up to par (a delightful irony that did not escape Morgan when forty years later he was invited to speak before a Methodist conference in Liverpool where part of the agenda had to do with admission of candidates to their ministry).

Years later, looking back on the experience, Morgan confided that he thanked God "for closing that door of hope, because, when He turned my feet in another direction I found the breath of His commandments, and the glory of His service."[2]

Although he would describe Methodism as his spiritual home, Congregationalism became his church affiliation. In the fall of 1890, Campbell Morgan was ordained into the Congregational ministry at the congregational church of Stone in England.

Many ministers confess later that first parishes are sometimes difficult because the new minister is still untested and the congregation sometimes unforgiving of any shortcomings. Morgan had not been at the Stone church long before he realized how divided the membership had been long before he arrived. He wrote: "In that church there were two factions, and their antagonism to one another almost amounted to a feud."[3]

By training and inclination, Morgan said his chief joy and gift was preaching; and he especially thrived with groups of churches or evangelistic endeavors. When he began to work successfully with a neighboring church that had asked for help, the Stone deacons were quite unhappy, sending him a letter saying they had received numerous complaints about his preaching elsewhere without their consent; they let him know that he was not to accept any additional invitations without their prior approval. In his journal, Morgan reacted to the deacons' letter with such words as "absurd . . . unreasonable . . . illegal." But before he resigned, he consulted an older friend who advised him not to do so but to wait it out, suggesting he should not be surprised at the "selfishness of religious people."[4]

He stayed but in 1891 received a call to serve a congregation in Rugeley, about fifteen miles away. He took a salary cut to do so but was glad to be away from what had continued to be a painful experience in Stone. Years later, he saw God's hand in the Stone difficulties and in his new ministry in Rugeley, "where I found people, the fragrance of whose love will be with me to the end of my days."[5]

It was a tremendous crisis in my life [rejection by Methodists]—the moment when the one string upon which I tried to play the music of my ministry stretched under the bow of life.[6]

Dear Mr. Morgan,

The Deacons held a meeting last night to consider several strong complaints which have been made to them respecting you, and the outcome of that meeting was the following unanimous resolution.

The Deacons having received several strong complaints concerning the Pastor's repeated absence, and one of these having taken a formal shape, they are constrained to desire Mr. Morgan not to accept any further invitations to leave his pastoral duties *without their consent*, as they are fully convinced that repeated absences are weakening and dividing the church.[7]

The Spirit guides, not by flaming visions always, but by circumstance, by commonplace things, by difficult things, by dark things, by disappointing things. . . . It is when man is in fellowship with the Lord that the disappointment and difficulty are under the guidance of the Holy Spirit.[8]

Harmony is concordant differences. That is to say the unity of the Church is concordant difference. . . . You have no right to speak of anyone as being a weak member of the Church. You have no right to say that, because a person is not doing your work and is not seen in the public places of the field, that, therefore, he is not doing the work which God would have him do. . . . It is not always the men and women who are at the front or in the pulpit who are God's greatest workers in the Church. In the vast majority of churches in London they could do better without the pastor, if they only knew it, than without the man or woman who prays in secret and never comes into the pulpit.[9]

> Workers together with him.
>> 2 Corinthians 6:1 KJV

Jesus Christ formulated no creed. I am more strongly convinced of that every day I live. There was no creed in His teaching. He did not . . . promise to any man an entrance into His Kingdom if his doctrines were orthodox. I am not saying a word about having our truths right and our doctrines pure; but, sometimes, I am afraid we put them out of order. . . . He lived amongst men, and taught men, and died for men, to put lives right, not their beliefs.[10]

By and large our ideas become so narrow that the walls of our sanctuary enclose them, and the roof crowns them. We are thinking of building Churches, not of building *the* Church. Jesus Christ never meant to build a place in which men should lull themselves into a sweet and happy slumber until the day of doom. He meant them to be gathered together into church life; but for what? Not merely for the purpose of worship, but also for the extending of His kingdom.[11]

But there is something before our business, before our pleasure, before our home—it is our position before God. When He came out amongst men, He found men were all wrong: there was discord everywhere. . . . And He not only found men were out of harmony with the music behind the veil but that they were rebellious; that they did not set their lives to the music of Jehovah, but they were in discord still.[12]

Characteristic in the work of Jesus Christ is His *self-abnegation*. There was no "Me" in it. . . . The words of the apostle when he was struck down on the road to Damascus must be those of every Christian worker: Lord, what wouldest Thou have me to do?[13]

My brother and sister, I am talking to you . . . I want to ask you, What has been your Christianity up to this moment ?
If you would be workers with Him, you must share His sorrows and His difficulties . . . to lift men up, to set the music right with the music behind the veil.[14]

A day dawns when God comes along and changes all the plans. . . . And God says, leave everything; depart from the place to which I brought you, and go.[15]

The government of God in its apparent contradiction is often perplexing. I believe that there are circumstances in this life of ours, through which some of us have passed, and may be passing now, that will never be explained so long as we remain here. If I personally attempted to explain my life by circumstances, apart from the assurance of divine over-ruling, I should be in despair. Is the government of God apparently contradicting His own arrangements? Then the one thing that is sure and certain is this, that in such hours He never leaves us. . . . If in the hour of our perplexity, almost despair, because it looks as though God is breaking up His own arrangements for us, we will seek His presence, He will talk to us. I do not know what He may say to you in detail. He ever says to us in such as this, wherever my changing plans may take you, I am going with you.

The things which perplex us are never really contradictory, but are contributory. I do not understand, but that does not say God is making a mistake. God changes my direction, crashing in upon my arrangements, the arrangements He made, the direction He indicated. I do not understand it. No, but bye and bye I shall. . . . Let us go forward taking the first word that God said to Jacob to our own souls. What was it? "Fear not, fear not." I am going with you wherever you go. I am over-ruling all your experiences, and moving forward with you toward the great finality.[16]

If a man does not do the will of God, as God requires it of him, step by step, and day by day, his belief is only thrown away. While we are fighting for our creeds, we are wasting the moments that are flying away. I pray God, He will never allow us to waste another moment fighting for a creed.[17]

I have been in eternity all along; but God hid it from my view. Then, Christ not only linked time with eternity, but also things temporal with things spiritual. Have we not been making a mistake, talking about things temporal and things spiritual? Are they not one? Does not the life on the other side of the veil depend on the life here? Not on the doctrines, not on the creed, not on the belief, but on the life? And should not this life be a preparation for the life that comes after? What did Christ mean when He said, "Seek first the Kingdom of God and His righteousness, and all these things shall be added unto you?" Did He not mean that the first business of every man and woman was to see that their life was right with God, so that, when they crossed the threshold to meet Him, there might be no discord, but harmony?

True. We must have pleasure—innocent, legitimate pleasure it may be. We must have a home life. . . . But there is something before our business, before our pleasures, and before our home—it is our position before God. Let us think of that. Christ had come out from behind the veil; He knew the notes that were struggling through; He noticed the music of the perfection of God. When He came out amongst men, He found men were all wrong; there was discord everywhere. . . . And He not only found that men were out of harmony with the music behind the veil, but that they were rebellious. . . .

There was no "Me" in it [the work of Christ]. He put Himself completely out of the question. . . . He never asked the question, "Will this please me?" or "Will that please me?" This must be a characteristic of a successful worker for Jesus Christ. Self must be put on one side. That is where I lack, where you lack, where we all lack. We all know it would be good to do such-and-such a thing, but we do not do it, despite all the terrible issues that hang on it.

He had no prepared pillow to pass way upon, but thorns on His brow and anguish in his heart. It was no soothing softness for Him; it *made* His sorrows. It was not music for Him. If you would be workers with Him, you must share His sorrows and His difficulties. Alas, I have no hope of all you becoming workers with God. Some of you will say, "Mr. Morgan is depressed," but God laid a burden of souls on my heart, and I cannot shake it off. I have no hope for all of you. Would to God I had! Is there no man here who, without making any noise, will say, "I will be a worker with Him, side by side with the world's Redeemer, to lift men up, to the music right with the music behind the veil?" Oh! Are there some here who will take up that position? God grant that you may, for His Name's sake.[18]

We have no right to undervalue our ministry in the Church, for the Head of the Church has marked it out for us. . . . There are many, however, to whom the Spirit of God has given a specific gift which they ought to be using for the upbuilding of the Church, and they are not using it. . . . There is something wrong in the organization of the Church. I believe that God has put me here. God has put you into the Sunday school class, as truly; God has put you into that mission work, as certainly; God has put you into that home, with no outward work—perchance cut off from it. God hath set the members and we have no right to say . . . I am not of the body.[19]

One is almost compelled to inquire . . . how it is that gifts, ministrations, and working are in conflict so often in Christendom today. If we were all taking our gifts from the Spirit and using them under the direction of the Lord, and in the energy of God, this great unity underlying the diversity would for evermore forbid conflict between gifts. . . .

There are diversities of gifts. Of what nature are these gifts . . . ? The word "gift" might be more literally translated "gratuity." We do not like the word gratuity; we are very much afraid of it. It seems to have, somewhere beneath it, the thought of pauperism. We must never forget that such is exactly our position before God, and it is precisely what this word does suggest with regard to every gift that can possibly be used in the service of God—something which grace bestows.

One of the greatest mistakes we could possibly make about Church order and work is to imagine that the picture of old is a cast-iron representation of what the Church is always to be.

"Where the Spirit of God is, there is liberty," and perpetually has He changed the gifts bestowed. . . .

The Church of God lives in the gifts of the Spirit and the abiding authority of the Head, and we never can do more injury to the Church or to the world than when we endeavor to perpetuate methods which are manifestly no longer powerful, simply because they have been so in the past.[20]

There are two realms of mystery which persistently assault the soul of man, and produce within it the sense of fear. They are those of the unknown future and the unfathomed past. . . .

There is not only tomorrow, but other morrows, the inevitable days that will multiply into years, and the persistent years that complete the period of our earthly sojourn. For all these we have our ideals, but we see the perils as we look ahead, and we ask ourselves what is going to happen?

Or, there is that other realm of mystery. We stand and seriously think, and attempt to grasp the present life, the suffering that abounds, the weakness of which we may be conscious, and the death that lies there ahead. . . .

What shall we do in the presence of these two mysteries?

The eternal God is in thy dwelling place, and underneath are the everlasting arms. What, then, does the word "eternal" mean? That which is ahead, that which is in front. It refers to the front of place, or of time.

We have curious notions about life, and we cannot avoid them. We talk of the future, and of the present, and of the past. Has it ever occurred to you that the real future is the past, and the past is the future? I do not expect anyone believes me, for it does sound so absurd. Yet take it another way. Life is a procession, whether it be individual life, or the history of humanity. The beginning of the procession is past;

it has passed us, it has gone on, but it is still there, still moving, the forefront of life, its initiation is not in the future, it is in the past.

The God of the beginning is not distanced from us by the running ages or years. He is there, but He is always the God of the beginning. He is the beginning of every day. He is the beginning of every age. He is the beginning of every life.

But He is our dwelling place. All that was involved in the beginning is persistent through the processes to the consummation. . . .

But "underneath are the everlasting arms." . . . The Hebrew word means absolutely, at the bottom. What is that? The lowest level, underneath. We go down and down. How far can we go? Plunge, sink, sink down, and at last what? The everlasting arms. . . . As low as your thinking can carry you, as low as your experience can take you, what will you find there? The everlasting arms.

What are we to do? Underneath are the everlasting arms. Nothing in the mystery of life, strange mystery, is unknown to Him; and there is nothing there with which He cannot deal. Underneath all suffering. He encircles our sorrows with His own; but in that there is no despair, no weakness. . . .

Yes, we shall sink away in conscious weakness, losing everything we have known; and we shall awake to find those arms are round about us, and death is the gate of life.[21]

3 When Loved Ones Die

Throughout his life G. Campbell Morgan faced many losses, beginning with the death of Lizzie, his twelve-year-old sister. He was only eight years old at the time and was deeply saddened because she had been his only playmate. As a child, Morgan practiced preaching his sermons to Lizzie and her dolls as his "congregation." Years later he would recall the night he left home weeping so he could visit her gravesite, staying there so long it led to a bout with pneumonia.

Of all deaths, the loss of a young child may be the most painful. In 1894, Morgan's ministry was full of promise at the Westminster Road Congregational Church in Birmingham, England. People were filling the regular Sunday services; he was already starting his soon-to-be-famous evening of Bible studies while also preaching elsewhere in England and Wales. Morgan's health took a turn for the worse, however, and he retreated to a small isle off the English coast to recuperate. It was here that he learned of the death of his young daughter, Gwennie, a loss he felt for the rest of his life.

He linked the death of his little daughter with that of his sister years before and noted that these losses never completely left him though he believed both children had been reunited in heaven. Whenever one of his own children were asked how many were in the family, they would respond there were seven, six on earth and one in heaven.

Morgan also experienced the losses of his father in 1907 and mother in 1911. And in 1914 his closest friend and ministerial colleague, Albert Swift, died suddenly from a coronary.

Morgan saw death as an enemy. He knew its terrible cost to those left behind. He was a survivor and, therefore, experienced firsthand what every human being understands about the brevity of life and the pain of losing loved ones, but he also trusted God's promises to those who love Him—that He would not abandon them in this life or the next.

Death is not robed in beauty. It is named an enemy. Its long, persistent power is realized. . . . Death to humanity is always hostile and hateful. . . . Death continues, age after age, century after century, defying every attempt that man has made to discover its secret and abolish it. . . . Death is the wounder of hearts. It is the assailant of faith; it is the challenger of hope. . . . The Christian conception of release does not rob the earthly side of its terror.[1]

The veil that divides us from the life on the other side seems to grow thinner as our dear ones pass within it. In hours such as these we are flung back upon God. . . . We need to remind ourselves that nothing that happens today has its full explanation here and now. Some day we shall see things in perfect Light, and then we shall understand. . . . I believe that whereas the gap will always remain and the sense of loss abide, as it does with me . . . you will be led into a place of quiet assurance that God is too wise to make any mistake, and too good ever to be unkind.[2]

I cannot tell, but this I know, that when my loved one lays down the body, that casket of clay is not my loved one. For forty-four years these eyes had looked down at one face with reverence and with love, and I looked at it for the last time on the last day of 1907, and I said, No, that is not my father. Dear sacred dust, very precious, but my father broke the fetter, and passed on. Oh, yes, says the materialist, everything was ending. No, says the Christian, the instrument was becoming imperfect, that is all. There are times when I cannot see quite clearly because the rain has fallen upon, or the fog has blurred the glasses that I wear. Do not blame me, blame the instrument. Thank God for the hour in which my father escaped from the worn-out medium of the earthly body, and went into life.[3]

I pass no day when I am not conscious of the nearness of at least one who entered into the veil sixteen years ago, my first lassie. . . . I know the touch of her spirit upon mine, for the spirit life cannot be measured by dimensions of the material. I know though she cannot come to me, I shall go to her. I have not lost my child; she is mine as never before. . . .

We still miss our loved ones, and we still shed tears. Our sense of loss is the result of what God has made us emotionally, and we should be less like God if we did not miss them. Our tears He never rebukes. . . . The sense of loss is not wrong when the loved one passes on, and I know I shall never again touch that dear hand until the morning of the resurrection.[4]

Let us remind ourselves . . . of the fact that the fear of death is not only widespread but it may be described as universal. . . . This fear of death still abides . . . even among the children of God, the children of light. Perchance it is the last fear to be overcome in the heart of the trusting saint, as death is the last enemy to be overcome. We are conscious of the chill of it even though we live in the warmth of the risen Sun of righteousness. . . .

May we . . . ask the reasons of the fear? What fills the heart with fear in the presence of death, either our own death or that of loved ones? First of all, let us remember that even if we believe man is immortal, it is still true that death is the passage from the familiar into the unfamiliar. We do not know what lies beyond; it is the borne whence no traveler returneth. We have all felt the terror of that as we have stood by the side of a loved one about to cross over. It is the leaving of the familiar and the reaching of the unfamiliar. It is the severing of associations, and the ending of fellowships. It is the interruptions of plans and purposes, and the cessation of endeavor. . . . These are the things which make men afraid. These are the reasons why man does so perpetually and so persistently fight against death.[5]

A telegram was put in my hands telling me that he [Albert Swift, his long time friend and ministerial colleague at Westminster Congregational Church] had gone! I could not believe it, and rang up on the telephone and spoke to his child. "Is it true?" I asked. She replied: "Yes, it is true. He was on his way to his garden." He reached his garden; but it was the garden of God, where flowers never fade, and which death never enters.[6]

Our Savior Christ Jesus, who abolished death.
                                                2 Timothy 1:10

We come to Easter morning with joy and gladness, and with a great sense of triumph filling our hearts. . . . This morning in our hearts there is the assurance that the winter is over and gone, and the time of the singing of birds is come. The storm has spent itself, the great Master Mariner is triumphant, and the Ark rides upon the waves of a sunlit sea. Egypt is behind, the exodus is accomplished. Death is abolished, life and incorporation are brought to light.[7]

Christ . . . has made death of no effect. He has made death void, empty. He has emptied death of all that which filled the heart with fear. . . . In His resurrection, He, the permanent, the continuous, the spirit, the essential, took His body out of the tomb, leaving the grave clothes absolutely undisturbed, and leaving the stone still in its place. . . . It was when John and Peter saw those undisturbed grave clothes that they believed He had risen. If they had seen the grave clothes carefully folded and smoothed they would have thought someone had stolen the body. . . . An angel rolled back that revolving stone that men might see He was not there . . . the touch of His spirit so transformed it that it was no longer subject to the laws which are only of the material, but became the spiritual body of which Paul speaks in his great Corinthian letter.[8]

If you really want to know what heaven is like, get any little bit of earth where Jesus is King, and you will see it. Do not be afraid of your imagination. Flowers? Oh, yes, immortals. . . . Birds and animals? Surely, yes; armies of white horses for the saints to ride upon? You say, "You are talking figures of speech." Quite probably so, but figures are used to help people to see facts that are too brilliant for their seeing. . . . No, the country beyond is not unfamiliar. I not only know it, I am learning its language. . . . I know men and women, saints of God who have walked and talked with Him for fifty years or more, and their accent is so much the accent of the other side that men call them foreigners. We know the country to which the loved ones have gone because we know the country's King.[9]

But if Christ did not rise, all is unutterable nonsense. . . . Do not imagine . . . you can deny the historic Christ and the historic resurrection. It is a miracle in the midst of the ages, not natural evolution. . . . Deny it and you have no comfort—the thud of the clod upon the coffin and that is all. But blessed be God, He is risen, we know He is risen.[10]

I hold most strongly that there is absolutely no warrant in Scripture for the medieval teaching concerning a hell of literal fire. . . . Christ never said anything which can be construed into the doctrine of the annihilation of any human being. . . . It is not permitted for us to know what passes between the soul and its Maker in the last hours of this probationary life. . . . No person will ever be separated from God for the rejection of Christ who has never heard His Name. Men will be judged according to the light they have had.[11]

To me the continuance of personality and the enjoyment of all its powers make it utterly inconceivable that there can be any other than the taking up on the other side of the communion, broken for a time, when loved ones pass over.[12]

Thus we must remember that the Christian doctrine of death is not in any sense cessation of being. It is rather separation. Physical death is the separation of the spirit from the body. Spiritual death is the separation of the spirit from God. The spirits of the just made perfect are more alive than they ever were, because they are more consciously with God. For them, being absent from the body is being at home with the

Lord, and that is life indeed. He is indeed the God of our loved ones who as to this earth have fallen on sleep, and that means that they are alive. By and by, in resurrection, they will awake, even in bodily form, in His likeness, and that will be their final perfecting.[13]

May God, the God of all comfort, send you home, especially you my beloved who are bereaved, not to be callous or indifferent, but to know that He gilds the teardrop with His smile and makes the desert bloom awhile; to know that He has your loved ones safe, and that when God comes, He will bring them with Him.[14]

The true quality of friendship is love, and the one expression of perfect friendship is that of adherence, loyalty, or . . . one who "sticketh closer than a brother" (Proverbs 18:24).

The heart of man is forever craving friendship. Let every man beware of the crowd of acquaintances. Let every man value at the very highest the friend who is a true lover. It is a little difficult in June days to distinguish between the acquaintance and the friend. We have to wait for November and December. It is not easy to know your friends when the sea is smooth and reflects heaven's blue. You will find them when the sky is overcast . . . and you are in peril.

The difference between acquaintances and friends is the difference between the reeds that grow by the river side and the rough, gnarled old oak stick when you are contemplating climbing hills. If I had a rough hill to climb, give me one rugged old oak green by the river bank.

The most lonely moment I ever had in my life was in 1896, when I first landed in New York. I stepped from the great steamboat on to the wharf, and there were hundreds of people meeting friends, but no one meeting me. Not a voice I knew, not a face that was familiar, and I stood for a few moments, feeling desolately lonely. I am never lonely now when I go there, but I was lonely for that first hour.[15]

I am prepared to say that no two men ever knew closer friendship than that which existed between Albert Swift and myself.

I met him . . . and that was the hour our friendship began. . . . There we talked of a common ideal, that of the ministry of Jesus Christ, and that of our desire to give our lives most unreservedly to Him so far as He should see fit to use us.

Then there came a crisis in my own life. . . . The great Methodist Church told me she had no room for me in her ministry. Albert Swift immediately gave up his position as sub-editor of a paper . . . and joined me in evangelistic work. For some time we traveled together, he arranging, organizing, and I preaching. . . .

In 1904 I was invited to Westminster. I knew I could not do the work; I at least knew some of my limitations; but I knew where the man was who, if he felt it to be the calling of God, would stand by me, and I was certain that we together could do the work. He was approached, invited; and he came.

Among all the days of our friendship none were more sacred than those days of the beginning of our work here, when with masterly skill he laid out the plans for all the organizations.[16]

Bereavements—I speak to you with all gentleness and all reverence, knowing that when a man treads the ground which is the ground of some sacred sorrow of bereavement, it is holy ground, and he should indeed put off the shoes from his feet; yet it is not right to sit alone with the memory of your dead while other souls in deeper sorrow are needing the help of your love. How long will you allow the tragedy of your own bereavement to paralyze your power to help others?[17]

Thomas Nicholson, who commenced his ministry in the same year that I commenced mine at Westminster . . . was to have stood at this desk and preached to my congregation. . . . A week ago . . . he retired to rest, and on the following Monday morning passed away from the earthly service.

How can a man escape from the oppression of these things? They are common enough, I know; I suppose no Sunday passes without there being some in this house who are face to face with the grim and ghastly fact of death. Perhaps, therefore, it is good that I should be compelled ever and anon to face it also. . . .

Whenever we come to the side of the grave, it is ours to set that grave in the light of the empty tomb in the garden of Joseph of Arimathaea, and to feel that there beats upon its barren darkness the waves of billows of eternal light. Therefore while death remains an enemy, the resurrection stands confronting it. . . .

Christianity also teaches us that the complete abolition of death is postponed. Until sin is cast out death cannot be cast out. . . . The last enemy that shall be abolished is death. In these words, the sequence of the campaign of Christ is suggested. He Himself having abolished death, in His own person, having appeared to those early disciples, and having constituted and formed His Christian Church, now reigns; and His reign is administrative, the application of the victory won personally to all the affairs of human life and through all the centuries. The conflict goes forward against sin, against sorrow, against disease, against limitation, against all those things that blight and spoil humanity. . . . Sin without death would be the cruelest fate that could overtake man. That is hell. Suffering without death would be the most brutal thing. Therefore man's natural death is retained until all other enemies have been subdued.

The risen Lord reigns over death. Death is no more outside His government. Death cannot come save by His permission. That is the Christian doctrine.[18]

4   Confronting Illness

Campbell Morgan confronted health issues most of his life. As a boy of eight, he ran grief-stricken to his only sister Lizzie's grave, desiring nothing but to join her in death. His parents found him unconscious, and he was later diagnosed with pneumonia and recovered only after a difficult struggle. In 1886, highly involved in many Salvation Army meetings and exposed to the rugged winter climate, Morgan developed throat trouble, which became a persistent, chronic problem. Morgan referred to it as "my old enemy."

In March of 1894, his throat trouble was aggravated by a neck tumor that needed surgery. In January of 1901, the "old enemy" recurred and resulted in a period of complete silence for two months. Later that year he had a second surgery. He praised the Roman Catholic nurse, Nurse Burgess, who had been a major factor in saving his life. Morgan described this near-death experience in his diary: "Ten years ago I was pastor of a church in North London. . . . Stricken, smitten and afflicted I came to the very borderline of eternity, spent a day and a night there, expecting to cross over."[1] Another health crisis caused Morgan to spend a month recuperating at Mundesley-on-the-Sea. Morgan wrote about this time of enforced silence and called it "Five Silent Sundays."[2] He found that experience mirrored in the twenty-seventh Psalm, when some serious illness caused anxiety that ended in faith. In the year 1914, Morgan suffered his major health crisis, which involved mental as well as physical suffering. Unknown to most people, Morgan suffered from malaria and burnout. In his "Nineteen Minutes of Reminiscences," he wrote: "The next reminiscence is that of a breakdown, failure in health, waning strength . . . and I was compelled to do what perhaps no one will ever realize what it cost me to do: lay down my work at Westminster and go out once more by faith."[3]

On September 26, 1914, Morgan preached a sermon titled "Ten Years" at Westminster that was greatly misunderstood. Jill Morgan, his biographer, wrote: "Campbell Morgan possessed an amazing resilience, but on the few occasions when serious illness attacked him, it struck with such force as would seem fatal. This time he had not the elasticity of youth with which to spring back, and only an indomitable will was left to help medical science fight the virulent disease. It was a long, hard pull even for a fighter, and it was Christmastime before he was able to take his place in the church."[4] Once again Morgan connected his story with a biblical story. His first sermon after his recovery was "The Psalm of a Convalescent." Morgan found his own story of sickness and recovery in the biblical story of King Hezekiah's remarkable recovery. Like the king, Morgan had found a new spirituality through his suffering. Morgan's lifelong struggle with illness made him solicitous and compassionate toward all who experienced illness, the night side of life. Morgan was never the theologian who propounded sublime truths that were never experienced, but the wounded healer, whose comfort came from the God who comforted him.

In 1894 I broke down in health in my Birmingham pastorate and had to go right away, in what seemed to be a most successful time of service, into the desert. My heart was hot, and restless, and rebellious, and the thought uppermost was that I was plunged suddenly into darkness, a darkness that was with me all the time. The very next morning after I went down to the quiet little seaside town in Wales, I took my Bible up in the regular course, and there came to me this verse, "I will give thee the treasures of darkness" . . . there came to me a message, which . . . was the revelation of the fact that God does give to those who are His, and who are following in the pathway of His appointing, even though of darkness, the treasures of darkness.[5]

I was still facing personal problems, without any clear, shining light. Then there came to me again words I had used writing on my second first day, "Unless I had believed to see the goodness of the Lord in the land of the living." And so I spent the morning thinking of the terrors of life, but finding them all transfigured in the glory of His goodness.[6]

Before going to the United States it fell to my lot to be suddenly smitten down in the midst of work very dear and precious to my heart, and for three long, and in many senses, weary months I was not able to touch my work. I found out what Paul meant when he spoke of the God of all comfort. God comforted me, not only directly but through His own people. It is a great thing for a minister to suffer if it is only to find out how tender people can be.[7]

I have known the desperate struggle against God, I have known what it has been to find His hand laid so heavily upon my life that life has become broken, helpless, and I have known what it is like to come to the morning that broke after the darkness, and say, "I have seen God face to face and my life is healed."[8]

> I had fainted, unless I had believed to see the goodness of
> the LORD in the land of the living.
>
> Psalm 27:13 KJV

The Psalm from which our text is taken is a song of conflicting emotions, in which the victory is on the other side of the nobler. As we listen to the singer we discover forces at war within his soul. Faith opposes itself to fear, joy strenuously contends with sorrow, songs resolutely lift themselves for the silencing of sighing. . . . The tumult of sorrow we know. Is the triumph possible? Is it possible to know triumph in the midst of such tumultuous circumstances of grief? We wonder, we question, we doubt. Our sorrows are so subtle, our pain is so poignant, our difficulties are so complex, our circumstances are so peculiar . . .[9]

The land of the living . . . is the place of weakness. There comes to us inevitably sooner or later the overwhelming sense of inability. We look back over the pathway we have traveled. We look at the things we have done, and looking back, we note how imperfect they have been. We look carefully at the things we are doing today, and the sense of imperfection is even more appalling. . . . Then we look on, and there are so many things to be done which we shall never do, intentions that will never be fulfilled, work that has to be dropped and left and cannot be carried out. . . . The appalling sense of inability, incompetence, weakness![10]

What light does this fact of God fling upon this strange, weird life of ours? How does it help us? In what sense does belief in this God turn the sighing into song, the fear into faith, the sorrow into joy? What are the things that make the triumph note of a song like this that thrills with pain? . . . We believe that all things which in themselves fill the soul with fear are held in the grip and grasp of the Great Father of infinite grace.[11]

Wait! There is nothing more difficult to do. It is much easier to work for God than to wait for God. To dare in active service is a far less wearisome thing than to wait, and yet by waiting the victory comes as well as the vision. . . . The outlook is that of the men and women who have looked at life, looked at it all; and who if they have had nothing other to look at than life, have grasped with horror, and been faint with fear. If such have believed to see the goodness of the Lord, then He teaches them this lesson, that in their waiting, they give Him opportunity to work. He worketh for him that waiteth for Him.[12]

For us, also, there is a past that we want to be dealt with; there is a future which is menaced by the past; and deeper than all others, there is the sense within our own souls, that we need some healing touch, some infinite and eternal medicine for the soul, that will make fever end and bring us new strength and peace. We need healing of life. Is that not the truth concerning ourselves?[13]

As to myself, sometimes it seems to me that I have been almost a perpetual burden upon you in recent years, with breakdown and failure of health. . . . All I know is that today I am weary, and weakened. . . . There is sadness, I say! And once again, there is anxiety; but it is only anxiety that we make no mistake about tomorrow, neither you, nor I. For you and myself I pray one prayer:

Jesus, still lead on,
Till our rest be won;
And although the way be cheerless
We will follow, calm and fearless;
Guide us by Thy hand
To our Fatherland.[14]

By these things men live.
Isaiah 38:16

The writing of Hezekiah is preeminently the Psalm of the Convalescent. . . . The Psalm was written in the days of convalescence, when, looking back, the whole of the facts were most plainly before his mind. Hezekiah had been stricken with sickness in stirring times . . . when as it seemed the most important work of his life was waiting to be done, the king fell sick unto death. In his distress he turned to God in sorrowful supplication. His prayer was heard and his life were spared. In the days of recovered strength he looked back, and this Psalm is the expression of what he felt as he does so.[15]

Affliction is that experience of the soul in which a man is brought to the end of self-confidence, because he is brought absolutely to the end of his strength. Sometimes the experience is wrought physically; sometimes without physical disease, it is wholly mental and spiritual. But whether by this method or by the other, the consciousness is that of the destruction of strength, of being weakened by the way, of being brought into that position where hope for the moment dies out. The great procession marches on without you; you are left wounded, halted, bruised, and helpless in the way. There is a sense in which hope is not dead in your heart. You believe the thing for which you hoped will yet to be achieved, but you yourself are left at the point where there is no more strength in you, and all self-confidence naturally and necessarily dies.[16]

"By these things men live." One of the first and supreme values of affliction is that it frees the soul from conventionality, enables us to realize things as they are, and thus compels us to speak with absolute freedom in the presence of God. . . . When the soul is stripped to stark nakedness it discovers itself . . . I pray those of you who do not perfectly understand me, to hear me patiently when I speak not so much of a theory as of an experience . . . when the soul is stripped to stark nakedness, when the robe of flesh though not yet dropped, is nevertheless so utterly useless that you can do nothing other than know yourself spiritually, the soul discovers itself.[17]

All the things upon which we have been dependent are gone; all the great work in which we have taken a part is left; and halting for a moment, we hear the music dying away, as the procession leaves us. Then when we are weak in soul and weary, when strength is at its lowest ebb; we begin to feel the tremendous and overwhelming majesty of our spiritual being. Then we find that God is nigh, and that we are still able to commune with Him; then it is that we find the meaning of that which comforted us, even in the days of health; Underneath are the everlasting arms.[18]

Are you afflicted, broken, bruised, left upon the highway while the great procession moves on? Let me say to you; Do not be afraid in this hour of loneliness. . . . Say all you think and feel to God. Then remember, that man lives by God's Word, and that so surely as you are walking by the way He leads you to the place where you utter the deepest things of your thought, He will answer you. He will speak to you . . .[19]

One of Morgan's last sermons preached at Westminster Chapel, London, August 8, 1943.

> The eternal God is thy dwelling-place, And underneath are the everlasting arms.
>
> Deuteronomy 33:27

Then, "underneath are the everlasting arms." Fears, yes, of life, the mystic elements of life, the surprises that come up within my personality, the good and the bad, the mixed motives. Of those we become more and more conscious as life hurries on to conclusion. Fears of suffering, its reason and value, not so much our own suffering, as that of others. Weakness, spiritual, physical, more. Is there any agony more poignant than physical weakness when we become so weak physically that we can lift no finger. . . . Underneath all suffering, He encircles our sorrows with His own . . . and in the last reach in the descent, we find His arms.[20]

Although Campbell Morgan believed all Scripture to be the inspired Word of God, there were certain passages that he dearly loved, as evidenced by how often he cited those texts. In this sense it can be said that this text was a "canon within the canon" for him.

> My grace is sufficient for thee.
>
> 2 Corinthians 12:9

This phrase forms part of a story in the life of one man. It is, however, a great word, revealing a profound philosophy of life, unfolding the deepest truth concerning God; in the knowledge of which life finds the place of peace and rest. . . . It is remarkable how these words have taken hold upon the heart of humanity. I think that as a general rule it is not wise to differentiate as the value of particular portions of God's Word, and yet there are outstanding passages which all men seem to know and love. These passages are characterised by simplicity of statement and sublimity of meaning. This is one of them. "My grace is sufficient for thee." Upon that great word many a weary head has rested, many wounded hearts have been by it healed; discouraged souls have heard its infinite music and have set their lives to new endeavour until they have become victorious. . . .

[This text] does not for a single moment suggest that the adverse circumstances are outside the Divine government. The meaning of the grace of God here is far more profounder, far more startling, and full of comfort, God is not saying that to His servant, It is very hard, and very difficult, and very trying; if it could have been avoided, it would have been better; but seeing that it could not have been avoided, I am with you, I am going to help you, strengthen you.

"My grace." What is the meaning of this great word? Who shall answer that question? The word runs through all the New Testament. We see it everywhere, first shining and flaming in revealed glory in the face of Jesus Christ. . . . The grace of God. The old theological definition of the word, that grace is unmerited favour, remember that is only a partial definition. Grace exists before it becomes a favour given to anyone. Grace is the fact of the heart of God. You may spell in the four great letters which give you the great word love. It is essentially the truth concerning God. . . . God finds His delight for ever more in loving, and in the presence of need, in healing and restoring and blessing.

First is this truth, that "God is love." He is a God of grace, therefore His arrangements for my life are all of love and are all of grace. Every pain that comes to me is a part of His economy, and therefore is a precious pain . . . when God had spoken to his soul, and he came to understand that the pain was also part of the Divine provision, he sang in the midst of it, triumphed over it, he rejoiced in it. He made the very suffering the reason for song.[21]

> About midnight Paul and Silas were praying and singing hymns unto God, and the prisoners were listening to them; and suddenly there was a great earthquake, so that the foundations of the prison-house were shaken: and immediately all the doors were opened, and every one's bands were loosed.
>
> Acts 16:25–26

What cannot be cured must be endured. I am afraid I have often said it, but when I have done so it was because for the moment I have forgotten my Christianity. What cannot be cured must be endured is paganism. It is wonderful that paganism ever climbed to that height. It is a great attitude, it is heroic up to a certain point, but it is not Christianity. Christianity does not say what cannot be cured must be endured, it says, rather, *These things must be endured because they are part of the cure.* These things are to be cheerfully borne because they have the strange and mystic power to make whole and strong, and so lead to victory and the final glory. Christianity is never the dour pessimism which submits. Christianity is the cheerful optimism which cooperates with the process, because it sees through suffering and weakness, joy and strength come. . . . Look back over the years. There they are, travel-worn years; much of light is upon them, but much of darkness also; many days of triumph, with the band playing and the flags flying, and many days of disaster and defeat. Already you know that the greatest things of life have not come out of the sunlit days, but out of darkened hours. Your sorrow has already been turned into joy. When your sorrow, that which was unendurable as it seemed at that hour, blossomed with beauty, your sorrow was turned into joy. Christianity as an experience is the ability to know that this will be so, even while the agony is upon us, and so we are able to sing in the midst of it. Men who sing while they suffer are men who have learned the profound secret that suffering is the method by which is perfected human life and history.[22]

Campbell Morgan and wife, Annie Morgan. Taken during his
sojourn in London during World War II. Morgan was 81.

5   When Tragedy Strikes

Campbell Morgan lived through many world tragedies, including two world wars. In his ministry at Westminster Chapel, two tragedies evoked special sermons: the sinking of the *Titanic* in 1912 and the outbreak of World War I in 1914.

On that fateful night of April 14, 1912, the seemingly unsinkable ship went down into a watery grave. The *Titanic* was the world's largest and most luxurious ocean liner. Yet, near midnight she met her doom when she suffered the fatal gash from an iceberg, and 1,503 people lost their lives. Morgan wrote, "The world is appalled by the disaster which has overcome the *Titanic*. It is so terrible that we are numb. All human enterprise is for the moment halted and humbled. . . . We can only pray for those desperately bereaved and that out of the tragic event some good may come."[1]

Morgan had personal reasons to reflect on the tragedy of the *Titanic*. Captain Edward J. Smith, who went down with the ship, was a personal friend. Another passenger who perished in the waters was Mr. W. T. Snead, a faithful member of Westminster. Another trusted friend and lifelong colleague was Mr. Harper, pastor of the Baptist church in Halworth. On April 25, 1912, Morgan preached a sermon entitled,

"The Wreck of the *Titanic*," which later appeared in the *British Weekly* and the *Christian World Pulpit*, as he struggled with the meaning of this tragedy.

All his life Campbell Morgan had been a committed pacifist. In a letter dated April 1914, four months before World War I began, Morgan expressed his disdain of war when he wrote, "I still hold that war is entirely contrary to the mind of God, and that it always arises from men being out of harmony with His mind and will. This was true in the case of wars chronicled in the Old Testament as in any other. . . . Had there been no corrupt nation there would have been no need for the fierce and terrible purging of war. . . . And so today, the whole war arises from human wickedness."[2]

Morgan's whole life had been devoted to peacemaking, so the war with Germany was a contradiction of all he believed and held dear. For five Sundays in August he preached a series of sermons on the war, which were later published in a little book, *God, Humanity, and the War*.[3]

Speaking of this struggle in later years, reflected in these sermons, Morgan said:

> They were preached in an agony. I am a lifelong pacifist, holding beliefs almost identical with Quakerism. I would never allow toy soldiers, even in my children's nursery. But my country had to enter the war and my work in that dark hour, was extraordinarily difficult. But the ministry of the Word is always needed, especially in the days of upheaval and breakdown in human affairs.[4]

The first sermon, "The Day of War, the Day of God," was preached on August 1, before the formal declaration of war. However, the following week saw Great Britain enter the war. In his second sermon of the series, preached on August 8, 1914, "The Life of Faith in the Day of Calamity," Morgan found it vital to support his country's entry into the war but continued to plead for the spirit of Christ for their enemies. On Sunday after Sunday, Westminster Chapel was crowded to the doors, until there was literally no room to sit or stand. "People lined the walls of the building, both upstairs and downstairs. . . . Even the large circular rostrum was crowded to such capacity that Dr. Morgan himself could barely make his way to the desk between the close rows of chairs on either side, and only had room to preach."[5]

Morgan's sermons were so dynamic that on several occasions the staid congregation broke into sustained applause—unprecedented in that stately sanctuary. Morgan's sermons made Westminster the rallying point for London in these grim days of August 1914. His final three sermons concerning World War I dealt with decisions that churches need to make, especially as peacemakers. He believed the church's response was a creative balance between grace and truth. Truth meant that this war could not be ignored and evil had to be resisted. Grace meant that those who fought in the war should not be condemned.

Jane Stoddard, assistant editor of the *British Weekly* magazine, reported the tremendous influence Campbell Morgan's sermon had on the people of London. "Dr. Campbell Morgan rose to his greatest heights as a preacher on the five August Sundays of 1914, before and after the declaration of war with Germany. Incomparable service was rendered by him at that time to the people of London, to the nation, and to the Allied cause."[6]

But for Morgan it was a pyrrhic victory. The strain of these sermons, compounded by a fever caused by malaria, led to his "resignation" sermon two weeks later.

Now there were some present at that very season who told him of the Galilaeans, whose blood Pilate had mingled with their sacrifices. And he answered and said unto them, Think ye that these Galilaeans were sinners above all the Galilaeans, because they have suffered these things? I tell you, Nay: but, except ye repent, ye shall in like manner perish.

Luke 13:1–3

I speak of some of the things that are in my mind in the presence of the catastrophe that has plunged the world for a moment into a sense of awe and of sorrow . . . I bring to you the piece of paper which has lain upon my desk, and upon which I have written things as they occurred to me; and here, in the midst of my people, I want to talk out of my hearing, being almost too overwhelmed to speak at all.[7]

Those of us who are Christian men and women need to be careful about what we say about this catastrophe. . . . This is not a divine judgment. We are face to face with the infinite mystery of the meaning and method of the Divine Government at such a time as this, and we are almost compelled to ask, "Why did God not interfere?" I have no detailed or immediate answer to that inquiry which satisfies my soul. My only answer is that from everlasting to everlasting He is God and that His acts are governed not by the cry of anguish of a moment, . . . but by the necessities of the processes which make for the realization of ultimate purpose. Beyond that I cannot go.[8]

To speak of this catastrophe as a judgment of God is to entirely deny the Biblical doctrine of God. The iceberg was the act of God; the *Titanic* was the act of man. Nothing, I think, can be more perilous in this hour, nothing more wicked, than any attempt to lay the blame for this catastrophe at the doors of any human being. May we be delivered from taking part in the sensational attempts to blame either the officers or the owners or any others.[9]

And now I propose to touch upon a matter which is even more delicate and more difficult. . . . It is the question of the spiritual life of those people who have been involved in sudden and amazing catastrophe; a question that will be largely asked by Christian faith whose standpoint and position is known as evangelical. The future of those who were suddenly overtaken and removed ushered into the life that lies beyond. . . . Let me remind you what the evangelical doctrine is, concerning the salvation of a human soul. . . . No man is ever accepted by God, no man is ever brought into the dwelling of light, because of Christian experience or fidelity. To put the matter in a brief sentence . . . forgive me if I express it personally, when at last I come to the end of service and life, whether that shall be by lingering illness, or God grant it, by sudden translation, when I stand in the presence of the light, and of the King, my language will be, "Nothing in my hand I bring, simply to Thy cross I cling." To be at home in the presence of God will not be the reward of my fidelity. I shall stand at last in the presence of the Throne, accepted in the Beloved.[10]

To me it is inconceivable that in those hours these men did not come face to face with eternity, did not realise the grandeur of their own essential spiritual life. And men so awakened are always awakened to the consciousness of sin; and men so awakening, inevitably and invariably cast themselves upon the mercy of God; and men so casting themselves upon that mercy are invariably accepted of God. To me there can be no doubt in the matter. I take you back to the old story of the malefactor on the cross by the side of Jesus, only one story in Holy Writ may no man be fool enough to presume upon the readjustments of relationships at the end; but one story that no heart need be filled with despair. And I believe that when in the light that lies beyond we shall review the things that have appalled and shaken our hearts to the very centre today, we shall discover multitudes who turned to God, and were kissed with the kiss of reconciliation and so found their way of His mercy into the life and love of the home that lies beyond.[11]

If we attempt to interpret this event in the terms of providence we shall tread very thorny and difficult ground. I am not denying providence. The doctrine of Providence is one I hold with all my heart and soul; but I should like to remind you . . .

> "There is a Divinity that shapes our ends,
>   Rough hew them as you may."

There *is* a providence watching over the affairs of men, controlling even the choices that are made in human freedom, not to immediate results, but to ultimate and final issues. I say there are quantities and facts and qualities of which we are ignorant, which must be taken into account if we are to have an accurate interpretation of providential dealings.[12]

[Morgan then told how Mr. Snead, a member of Westminster, was on his way to America to initiate a new interest in religious matters and he drowned. He mentioned a good friend Mr. Harper, who on his way to the Chicago Bible Institute for three months of lecturing, also perished. Morgan's friend Stuart Holden had booked passage on the *Titanic*, but his wife's illness prevented him from the voyage.] God is good, and often His ways are:

> ways in which we cannot tell;
> and He hides them deep,
> like the bidden sleep
> of those He loves so well.[13]

When Tragedy Strikes

The accidental method of physical ending of a life is nothing; the supreme and essential fact and matter of urgency in every life is the relation of that life to God. So may we hear this great spiritual word. While we shall turn our attention . . . to all the lessons which we are to learn to the conserving and making safe of human life . . . and what we shall give with generosity and even with sacrifice, and care for those who are bereft, and left us sad, let us not shut our ears to the voice of the Master, but make this an opportunity for turning to God with true and godly repentance and yet with loving fear.[14]

> The LORD will give strength unto his people; the LORD will bless his people with peace.
>
> Psalm 29:11

We are gathered together under the shadow, which is almost more than a shadow. The deep ensue darkness of approaching and most inevitable calamity—the calamity of war. . . . I know nothing definitely; and yet I know enough as I stand here that the darkness of this evening is more pronounced than the morning. We are all waiting for events and we are conscious of the high tension thus created within our own souls . . . no one wants war; we do not want war in England; even those who hold it necessary do not desire it; I do not believe for one single moment that Germany, in its deepest heart desires war.[15]

Some force, impalpable, spiritual, devilish, seems to be attempting to compel war, confusing the issues, paralyzing our senses; stirring our animosities. What of the women and children of these nations? What of their men who will be marched like dumb cattle to slaughter?[16]

71

The Lord is king! Let the earth rejoice, let the many coastlands be glad! Clouds and thick darkness are all around him; righteousness and justice are the foundation of his throne.

Psalm 97:1–2 NRSV

Our country is now at war; we are at war after the most strenuous efforts for peace; our sons are marching to blood death; our women and children are smitten and stricken; desolation and death are with us. . . . I have preached from this pulpit for ten years, and you, my people, know how every vestige of my nature hates war. . . . Yet I am convinced that to have remained neutral would have been to disregard the obligations of national morality.[17]

I say unto you, "Love your enemies, and pray for those that persecute you"—the peoples against whom we fight are our fellow men. One thing upon which we must be firmly resolved—never again can a handful of men be able to speak the word that will involve the slaughter of millions at their will.[18]

The cleanest place in the war of 1914 will be the field of blood, where men, heroic and daring, fall and die! The most corrupt place is the spiritual darkness in which these shambles were made possible. There is the true region of horror; and into that realm the Church is called, in order to grapple with the forces of evil, that have made the actuality possible and even necessary, and in order that the thing that all men are saying in one way or another: Never again can this thing happen![19]

For our struggle is not against enemies of blood and flesh, but against the rulers, against the authorities, against the cosmic powers of this present darkness, against the spiritual forces of evil in the heavenly places.

Ephesians 6:12 NRSV

We must enter into the warfare by getting into grips with the foe; by putting ourselves in evidence as against anything and everything which tends to weaken the moral fiber of our people, to disturb their mental and spiritual strength . . . by seeking close comradeship with the tired and distressed; by standing side by side, in sane and happy fellowship with those who may be in peril.[20]

> What is man, that thou art mindful of him? And the son of man, that thou visitest him?
>
> Psalm 8:4

For the sake of brevity, let me make the illustration personal. Those who know me best, who are most familiar with the tones of my voice, the tricks of my hand, the sound of my footfall, do not know me. What is true of one lonely, isolated individual who now occupies the place of the preacher is true of every man that is marching with millions at the moment. These lonely and individual men are seen massed, as ammunition on one hand, and as bulwarks upon the other. . . . So I come back, as we all come back, to the sadness of the night, and to the silent fear of the morning newspaper, God grant that the light of this biblical revelation may be upon it. . . . God forgive us if we forget the tragedy of men slain! I care not whether they be German or British. Men slain! O! It is a horrible business. I pray that in these hours of strain and anxiety, when national warfare must have its way, that we as Christian people never lose the sense and horror of the murder of men, sons of their mothers—nay, sons of God! God deliver us from becoming callous in the presence of the awful horror of races antagonistic which should be serving each other! Yet look again, and see the hope of today. Is there any hope? Yea, verily, there is for me at least. I am not sure of anything except that God is reigning. Light is breaking. I cannot help but believe that out of this awful hour there will be an emergence of the consciousness of the sacredness of human life individually.[21]

> Multitudes, multitudes in the valley of decision! For the day of the LORD is near in the valley of decision.
>
> Joel 3:14 NASB

Finally, and in the briefest of words, the matter which we now decide, that is almost decided, concerns the secrets of Peace. They are not armaments, These do not make for peace, they make for war. . . . The men that have argued that there can be an armed peace, are finding themselves mistaken. No, a thousand times, no! The secrets of peace are not to be found in Alliances based on suspicion. These foster antagonism, and they are for War. Barbed wire is never friendly!

What, then, are the secrets of Peace? I take you back to an old song, the song and the anthem that we have rejoiced in once a year at Christmas, even since we were born. I pray that you will hear it again in this evil day, "Glory to God in the Highest; and on earth peace."[22]

Apparently many had asked Campbell Morgan about the future of servicemen who died fighting in World War I.

What comfort do we have for those who have no assurance that their loved ones were believers. This is the question of many troubled hearts today; a perfectly natural question, one forcing itself upon the thoughts, as many have fallen in battle. . . . There is a Scriptural answer to the enquiry. It is an answer which takes us far, and there halts us, and it is such an answer that halting, where it takes us, we may rest in perfect quietness. The answer is to be found in the simple evangelical faith of the Christian Church. The souls of men are received by God in response to their venture of faith in Christ Jesus.[23]

> Peace, I leave with you; my peace I give unto you: not as the world giveth, give I unto you. Let not your heart be troubled, neither let it be fearful.
>
> John 14:27

In these terrible days of war, when faith, if it not be shaken, it is certainly assaulted, we hardly know how to pray. There is however, one prayer which we all offer, continuously, earnestly, and with passionate desire. It is the prayer for peace. That prayer means most simply, and most constantly, that we long for the end of strife, the carnage, the suffering, the outrage on everything that is high and noble in human thought and feeling. . . . We must pray and work and fight, therefore, for a peace that means the ending of things that prevent peace, the ending of things that makes for war. We must strive for the ending of the delusion that one race has the right to rule over another by oppression, whatever that race may be; for the ending of the philosophy that brute force is the sanction of sovereignty.[24]

> Of his kingdom there shall be no end.
>
> Luke 1:33

The darkest hours in the history of the Church, and therefore of the Kingdom, have always been the hours leading on to new triumphs; and events which have seemed to conspire to crush His powers, have always been discovered as those by which He has most surely advanced toward more certain victory, and the possession in actuality of more of the territory which by right wholly belongs to Him.[25]

He shall not be afraid of evil tidings: his heart is fixed, trusting in the LORD.

Psalm 112:7 KJV

This is supremely a day of evil tidings. Our newspapers are full of them. They contain nothing else. Their good news, the news for which we look, and which comes to us ever and anon, is always laden with anguish. Battles mean hearts broken. This tide of sorrow is rising higher and higher in the nations, and its dark waters are overflowing into every hamlet and every home. But they are especially emphatic, these newspapers of ours, about the tidings which are wholly evil. They tell us that the Government is incapable and weak, that politicians are blind, that generals are incapable; or they summarise that all the wise men are out of office. . . .

The heart is fixed. Men who are strong are always men who are fixed somewhere, who have a conviction from which they cannot be separated by argument, which cannot be changed, whatever the circumstances in which they live. Sometimes these men are very narrow, but they are wonderfully strong; they are singularly obstinate but they are splendidly dependable. Consequently, we always know where to find these men. The fixed heart is the secret of courage. Courage is an affair of the heart; courage is the consciousness of the heart that is fixed. . . . What, then, shall we do in the day of frightfulness! We shall do our duty; the thing that is nearest; the thing we have to do tomorrow morning. We will do that, and do it well; and do it cheerfully. The rest we will leave to Him of sorrow, and suffering, and of the issues. What this nation needs now just as much, and perhaps more, than anything else, is the multiplication of strong, quiet souls who are not afraid of evil tidings, even though the Zeppelins may be coming, and will not add to the panic that demoralized, but will do their work.[26]

This is a sermon preached after the death of King Edward VII in 1910. At first Morgan was only to say a few words and then offer prayer, but he decided to speak from the heart, with no previous preparation—an unusual experience for him.

We are gathering together this morning under the shadow of a grave national loss. For nine years the throne of our beloved land has been occupied by a man who has proved himself to be a great King, constitutional, human, with great tenderness and sympathy, the nation's greatest asset in all matters of international outlook. And it is impossible for us to gather together in that worship of God which is at the very centre of our own life without recognizing how great our loss is . . .

The word that comes to my heart again and again is a word from the first epistle of John, in his second chapter, and the seventeenth verse, "The world passeth away, and the lust thereof: but he that doeth the will of God abideth for ever." And, as I may be helped, perhaps only for a few minutes, or as the guidance of the Spirit may be, I will say the things that are in my heart . . . I am quite conscious that this congregation is largely here as a result of the national consciousness at this moment. I believe that very many of you have turned in here to worship with us are here incidentally because we are near to the Palace where the king lies dead; but you are here because this is a House of Prayer, and you desire that your hearts should be reminded of those abiding and eternal things that know nothing of change and decay. . . . We are all reminded in such an hour of the transitoriness of human life, and I feel that the sense of the solemnity of that fact is upon us all. . . .

To the man who but yesterday or the day before passed to death, whether the King or the peasant or the pauper in sure and certain relationship of the will of God, death was robbed of its terrors. . . . The King who has passed over into the life that lies beyond may have other service to fulfill, but the great opportunity of this life's service is over for him. What he has written, he has written; what he has done, he has done. . . .

We turn from the thought suggested by the death of a King to the fact of our own lives. . . . Now listen, again, If you or I, my brother, my friend shall before next Sabbath day have dropped out of our place in this world, and have crossed the line, and gone to the larger life, the thing we do today—shall remain here, whether a lie spoken or a truth. Uttered, whether a kind action of love, or an unkind word spoken: whether it be a contribution to the healing of humanity's wounds or a blow that makes the wound more terrible, these things abide when we are gone. . . . With a fine and apt and beautiful fitness many of our papers have described him as Edward the Peace-maker. . . . May God by his grace purify and purge the words spoken this morning, and may He speak to us so much as may be through these words, but beyond them and beside them may we hear what God is saying to us in the hour of national visitation for His name and mercy's sake. Amen.[27]

G. Campbell Morgan responded to several letters, when World War I broke out in 1914, and these are some of his answers.

I have no other claim, and no other merit. My venture of faith in the love of God, and in the work of Christ, is the way of my salvation. Over the borderline there will be progression for all of us, tarrying places, lessons to be learned, instructions to be given. Those who are gone, have not come to final and absolute maturity of spiritual apprehension. They are being trained and taught. . . . My brothers and sisters, leave them with the God of the infinite mercy, out of whose tender heart of compassion all your anxiety has come. You and I can never think too well of God. Everything in us that makes us hope and long for the safety of those loved ones is in us because God's love is in us. So we may rest about multitudes, leaving them with Him.[28]

I still hold that war is entirely contrary to the mind of God, and that it always arises from men being out of harmony with His mind and will. This was true in the case of the wars chronicled in the Old Testament as in any other. Had there been no corrupt nation there would have been no need for the fierce and terrible purging of war. And so today, the whole war arises from human wickedness.[29]

I have been a peace man . . . all my life . . . at the present minute, however, while not having changed my views by an iota, it is quite evident to me that if England has not, in the present crisis, unsheathed the sword, she would have violated every principle of righteousness in the matter of international relationships.[30]

G. Campbell Morgan, a man of the Word, 1940, age 77.

6   Dreams Deferred

From all outward appearances, G. Campbell Morgan's ministry was thriving during the middle years of his life from 1904 to 1917. When he came to Westminster Congregational Church in London in 1904, the church had less than two hundred members. The members hardly filled the large and somewhat shabby auditorium of the sanctuary. During his ministry and with the support of his close colleague and friend, Reverend Albert Swift, the congregation grew not only in number of members but in the wider ministry of the teaching and preaching Campbell Morgan felt to be so important—ironically the very activities objected to so strongly in his first parish.

Morgan's working motto was always "a minimum of organization for a maximum of work." With Swift tending to the organizational work and he to the preaching and Bible studies, Westminster came alive. As the church grew, Morgan also extended his ministry outside the congregation by setting up a summer Bible conference center on the English coast, conducting evangelistic outreach in England, Wales, and the United States, and for a period of time serving as president of the Cheshunt College at Cambridge, where he helped raise funds for a building program for this Congregational seminary.

When Swift left in 1907 to become pastor of a church in Reading, England, Morgan felt the loss deeply, of not only the organizational support needed so he could focus on preaching and teaching but the close friendship. He still lectured widely in six circuits around England while also serving as president of the World Sunday School Convention, and even traveling to Rome. Of course, during this time his writing prospered with the publication of many of his sermons. However, while all this was transpiring, Morgan's health was not faring as well as his service to others.

In 1913, a number of difficulties arose. Morgan's eldest son suffered from a lung disease and moved to North Carolina to regain his health. In December, Morgan learned of Albert Swift's death. Later, a ten-day illness required him to give up his seminary presidency and focus his energy on preaching, which he did, including a series of Bible conferences in the United States. In 1914 war broke out.

September 27, 1914, was the tenth anniversary of his ministry at Westminster Congregational Church. On October 2 he gave a sermon entitled "Ten Years at Westminster" that was to shake his congregation and, indeed, the wider religious community. It was to be a very frank and personal sermon spoken to friends and members of the Westminster church. No one realized that day that on the following Sunday Campbell Morgan would hover between life and death as a result of a bout of typhoid fever.

It was Christmastime before he was able to visit any church, and not until February 1915 that he returned to the Westminster pulpit, having reconsidered his decision to leave. But in 1917 he resigned a second time from his Westminster ministry, perhaps feeling that though more was still to be asked of him, his dreams for Westminster had been deferred. Little did he realize then that in 1933, at the age of seventy, he would return to Westminster to serve as minister once again.

The text of a sermon G. Campbell Morgan preached on October 2, 1914, to explain his resignation from the Westminster Church pastorate.

I have seen an end of all perfection; But thy commandment is exceeding broad.

Psalm 119:96

My relation with this Church as its minister dates from October 1, 1901. . . . The last Sunday of September, 1914, is the last, therefore, of the tenth year of my work here. Ten years have gone, and in their passing they have added many more then ten to my own sense of age. If the saying be true that a man is as old as he feels, then by comparison, I am at least twenty years older, than when with a heart full of help, I took up this work, at the invitation of the Church here, which I found, few in numbers, but rich in faith.

It seems to me that this is a not inappropriate occasion for saying to my people some of the things that are in my mind and heart. . . . I propose, not so much to preach, as to talk, freely and frankly, as among friends. . . .

It is now about two and thirty years since I was first arrested by this text. I certainly then did not understand it; but I was impressed by the quiet and confident way in which it was quoted, and also by the effect it produced upon the one to whom it was addressed.[1]

Two men were standing talking together, having just left a session of a religious convention. The men were Robert Chapman, of Barnstaple, and my own father. They were troubled by certain religious and theological tendencies of their day, and after discussing them, Robert Chapman looked with clear eyes into the face of my father and said "I have seen an end of all perfection; but Thy commandment is exceeding broad."

My father lived for five and twenty years after that conversation. . . . No text was more often on his lips. Today I think I understand it. It seems to have become my own in a peculiar sense. . . .

The words occur in this most wonderful Psalm, which celebrates the goodness, acceptability, and perfection of the will of God as the law of human life. From the beginning to the end of the two and twenty alphabetical strophes of which the Psalm is composed, there is a note of sadness. That note, however, is all the time resolved into perfect harmony by the tones of confidence and triumph. . . .

The first part of the text has the unmistakable note of sadness: "I have seen an end to all perfection." By that the singer meant: I have seen the limit, the extremity, the breaking off, of completeness. I have seen that completeness, perfection, is unrealizable; the things of life are perpetually broken off, incomplete; perfection is unattainable. The city is not built, the dream is not realized, the ideal is not attained.[2]

This is the language of disillusionment; and if there is nothing more to be said, it is the sincere but disappointed wail of pessimism. . . . But there is something more to be said and this is it: "Thy commandment is exceeding broad."

By that the singer meant: Thy government . . . is exceeding roomy, spacious. Thy overruling of life, provides for more than the things which appear. The unfinished city is to be built; the unrealized dream is to materialize; the unattained ideal is yet to be fulfilled. Not here, not now; not, perchance in the way we planned; but none the less surely. . . .

No young man wrote this. It would be unhealthy in youth. Of course, I did not understand it two and thirty years ago! In spite of all our poetical figures, youth is not climbing the hill, it is descending into the valley. It is the old man who is climbing the hill. . . .

But that climbing man is seeing more. He is seeing the broad commandment of God, with its promise of sure ultimate spiritual realization; so that while he knows hope deferred, which has made sick his heart, he has now a new hope in God, which presently will be lost in sight, when faith in full fruition dies. . . .

There are three things I want to say to my own people. . . . They are things of my own heart. . . .

1. Had I foreseen the experiences through which I have had to pass during these ten years, under no circumstances would I have come. "I have seen an end of all perfection."
2. I thank God that I did not foresee, and that therefore I came. "But Thy commandment is exceeding broad."
3. I am at the parting of the ways, and I do not know what my future ought to be. "I have seen an end of all perfection," and therefore I have no panic.

I confine myself entirely to the things of the work here at Westminster; and inclusively I declare to you that during these ten years I have known more of visions fading into mirage, of purposes failing of fulfillment, of things of strength crumbling away in weakness, than ever in my life before.[3]

The fundamental plan was that of building up here a New Testament Church . . . a Church which should be evangelical and evangelistic; a Church which should be catholic and missionary, a Church which should be in the true spiritual sense of the word, a House of God. . . .

I think of the Church itself. Our membership is so scattered and the location of buildings is so peculiar, that our Church is by no means independent of the presence and ministry of one man.

The Schools . . . are understaffed and badly housed. . . .

All I know surely is that today I am weary, and weakened. . . . Whatever else Westminster has done for me, or has failed to do, it has certainly brought me very definite disillusionment in many ways.

That, however, is not all the story. This is the rest of it, and this is the best of it! "But thy commandment is exceeding broad."

During these ten years I have at least loved and sought to know and to do, the will of God. I may have missed the way more than once; I may often have failed to do the will; but no man shall take from me the confidence that in my deepest soul I have loved it, and so have desired to do it.

I realize today that the ten years of Bible teaching have produced results which cannot be tabulated, and which are far in excess of anything I could have imagined.

The . . . Bible Conference, which has been held for nine consecutive years, is the child of this work; it has steadily grown in numbers and interest, and the streams of its influence have run through all the earth.

Our Bible Teachers Association in which we have today an enrolled membership of 300 or 400 men and women who are regularly teaching the Bible is the outcome of work at Westminster. . . .

Students here have passed through our Friday classes, and have gone here and there and everywhere in this land and to the ends of the earth. . . .

There are a few mails that come from distant parts of the world that bring messages telling of help received from the publications that have gone forth from this place in ten years. . . .

I rejoice greatly, too, in the true catholicity of our work here. The members of all branches and sections of the one Church have found fellowship with us, over and over again, in our study and teaching of the Word; and often, too, as we have gathered in all simplicity around the Table of our Lord.[4]

End the ministry; disband the organizations; raze the buildings to the ground; but the spiritual work will live! Not because of the excellence of anything I have been able to do, for my plans have been broken, my ideals are unrealized, and I have seen the end of all perfection; but because His command is indeed exceeding broad [5]

And now for a few moments . . . I turn this backward look. What shall I say about tomorrow!

First, I have to say that I have no plans. I see many things that might be done. If the day of vision is gone because I am no longer young, the day of dreaming is not over, for old men dream dreams. If, however, I see many things that might be done, it is equally true that I see no way of doing them. Therefore I have to be content to know that they will not be done by me.

The second thing I have to say is that I have no panic. The broad commandment of God cannot fail. If it should be that my work at Westminster is finished, done in its incompleteness, well, so be it. . . . It also is a contribution to the final victory; and there my heart will be content to leave it.

If I have to say that I have neither plans nor panic, I want to say another thing, and I desire to call you into sacred and prayerful sympathy when I say it, I have serious problems.

One thing is now quite certain and established, and that is that the whole of my life work must be reconstructed. The question confronting me with almost appalling intensity of concern as the hours pass by, is as to whether in the will of God this is to be the place of its continuity? The question is being forced upon me as to whether it is worthwhile to preach constantly at one centre, where it is not possible to work out the teaching into the life of the church.

There is sadness. I have seen much disillusionment. Things are not as I hoped they would be in any single department of the work.

But there is a great gladness in the heart. I have made the great discovery of the supreme breadth of the Divine commandment.

Therefore, . . . it does not matter that things are not as I hoped they would be. Let the piece of work done drift out, let it pass into the eternities with its unfinished columns, its unrealized aspirations, its unfulfilled ideals. Ah! But there is a broad commandment of God, which will reconstruct and finish and bless. He will incorporate it, in the great whole of His glorious purpose. That is my comfort as I look back, and on.[6]

I am conscious of my own weariness and weakness. I am yet more conscious of the overruling of that weakness. It has been made the instrument of revealing the love and loyalty of my people in the most remarkable way. . . .

Great principles are involved; principles of life and service as within the broad commandment of God. Being within that commandment, nothing can be a failure, however disappointing it may seem. To miss the way of the Divine will, is indeed to fail, and that in spite of every appearance of success. Therefore, the question equally for me and the Church is not that of personal inclination or desire, but that of the will of God. . . .

There is sadness . . . there is gladness . . . and once again, there is anxiety. But it is only anxiety that we make no mistake about tomorrow, neither you nor I. For you and for myself I pray one prayer: Jesus, still lead on.[7]

The text of a July 2, 1915 sermon in which Campbell Morgan spoke about why he had remained at Westminster Church.

And now, O Jehovah God, the word that thou hast spoken concerning thy servant, and concerning his house, confirm thou it forever, and do as thou hast spoken.

2 Samuel 7:25

These words of David seem peculiarly suitable to me today. Indeed, I have chosen them, as giving expression to the language of my own soul at this hour, and that not only because of what they say, but also because of the circumstances under which they were uttered. This confession on my part will at once reveal the fact that I am going to speak in a very personal and intimate way, as to my own people—that is, to the people it has been my privilege to serve in the ministry of the Word now for nearly eleven years. . . .

Exactly eleven years ago today . . . I stood in this pulpit of this sanctuary and announced acceptance of the invitation which had been extended to me to become the minister of the Church here. This morning I am here to say that the resignation which under stress of strong conviction I placed in the hands of the Church, I have been compelled to withdraw under the irresistible pressure of the conviction of others.[8]

That which I desire, I cannot have. I am content, therefore, now to seek, so far as in me lies, to serve God and my generation in a way which my . . . friends feel is the best for me. When I was young, I girded myself, and walked whither I would; but now that I am old, I stretch forth my hands and others gird me and carry me whither I would not! Nevertheless, I hear the same Voice that spoke to Peter saying to me: "Follow me." And I know that to be a command to march through whatever may appear to be a land of shadows toward the place of light and power.[9]

Seated is George Morgan, G. Campbell Morgan's father, Baptist minister from Wales. Standing is Campbell Morgan (L) and Percival Campbell Morgan, oldest son. Three preachers of the Word. 1906.

Left to right: Howard Moody Morgan, youngest son,
Campbell Morgan at age 65, and Richard Morgan,
grandson. Taken in Lexington, Kentucky, in 1932.

7 Growing Older

The year 1913 brought troubled times for G. Campbell Morgan. He grieved the loss of his friend and colleague, Albert Swift, who had stood by him in the early halcyon years at Westminster Church. Working together, they had "great and glorious success." Morgan's ideal for the proclamation of the Word and social ministry in London was being realized. On December 9, Morgan reached the age of fifty, which was considered getting old in those days. Then the sad news arrived that Swift had suffered a serious coronary attack. Furthermore, the signs of an approaching catastrophe that would engulf Europe were all too obvious.

On December 7, Morgan preached a sermon on "Fifty Years—and Beyond." There is little doubt that Swift's illness (he died ten days later), and Morgan's own fiftieth birthday was on his mind and heart. For many years this sermon lay hidden in the archives of the chapel. Morgan, feeling his own weakness and depletion of energy, used the "retirement" of the Levites from their work in the tent of the meeting. The tent of the meeting is analogous to the tabernacle that the Israelites carried in their wilderness wanderings. The function of the Levites from age twenty-five to fifty was to transport the tabernacle and its furniture when the camp moved; when the camp rested, they had to erect the tent, take care of it, and assist the priests in their varied work. At fifty, they retired from these duties but could assist their brothers and offer wisdom in a teaching capacity. Morgan described how the Levites still could do voluntary work, assisting the priests in their teaching ministry. In a matter of a few years, Morgan emulated their model, as he resigned from Westminster and sailed for America. He laid down the burden of the pastorate in order to become an itinerant preacher and teacher of the Bible across America and Canada.

However, in 1933, at the age of seventy, Morgan returned to Westminster, London, as co-pastor with Dr. Hubert Simpson. Due to Simpson's poor health and later retirement, Morgan became senior minister again for four years (1934–1938). In the span of those years, and even later, the Friday night Bible school drew two thousand persons every night, hardly a "retirement" for Morgan. People still hungered to hear this Bible teacher expound the Word.

Due to Morgan's loss of strength in later years, Dr. Martyn Lloyd-Jones became co-pastor in 1939. Morgan finally gave up the pulpit in 1943, at the age of eighty. On May 16, 1945, he died peacefully at St. Ermin's Hotel in London, with the tower of Westminster Chapel in full view.

In a real sense, Campbell Morgan exemplified the words of the apostle Paul.

> So we do not lose heart. Even though our outer nature is wasting away, our inner nature is being renewed day by day.
>
> 2 Corinthians 4:16

The sermon, "Fifty Years—and Beyond," reflecting on the retirement of the Levites was published, but little remembered . . . until now. It has amazing relevance for the twenty-first century, an age when people's life spans are lengthening. Despite living in the midst of the Age Wave, with medical science and technology extending life beyond what was possible in Morgan's years, his words still resonate with us. As we age, we suffer similar losses and realize similar gains. This sermon once again powerfully demonstrates how Campbell Morgan's words still speak to a major issue of our time.

> And from the age of fifty years they shall cease waiting upon the work, and shall serve no more, but shall minister with their brethren in the tent of the meeting, to keep the charge, and shall do no service.
>
> Numbers 8:25–26

The Levites were representative men . . . at fifty he [a Levite] was released from the routine work, no longer taking place in the regular course of the Levites as they came up to the house of the Lord, and being set free from more exacting duties which made demands upon his physical strength. Thus he was able to render voluntary ministry in the holy place and things, and more distinctive functions. The work of the Levites was not merely that of ceremonial observances, but of the teaching of the law; and at the age of fifty he was set free for the fulfillment of this more distinctly and directly spiritual function.[1]

In the ancient world there were abiding values . . . a revelation of at least two principles in which we all do well to heed . . . the first is found in the recognition of the change that comes to a man at fifty years of age; and the second is found in its suggestion as to the nature of the service which is to be rendered from that time . . . it may once be said that some men are fifty at thirty; and some hardly thirty at fifty.

The thought of the text is that of middle age, when physical powers are losing their resilience, their buoyancy, their recuperativeness.[2]

What are the things that I have lost? First of all, the power of recovery. Recovery from weakness does not come so quickly as it did. Recovery from sickness is not so rapid as it was. Recovery from wounds is not so easy as it was, especially the wounds of the soul. . . . The buoyancy is gone, the old resiliency is departed, and one begins to understand . . . that all tiredness is the touch of death, which if it is pressed too far, will become death.[3]

We have lost a great deal of self-confidence. . . . We tremble a little more in the presence of new enterprises. We halt a little longer before we make a venture. We are not as sure, as we once were. . . . We have lost much of the old power of resistance. . . . We suddenly find ourselves, as we are pressing toward the scar and yellow leaf, assaulted by temptations that we thought forever had lost their power. We cannot resist, as we once did.[4]

Once again we have lost much of our sense of wonder, of our capacity for wonder. When I was a boy I lived for awhile with my father and mother and my one and only sister on a street called Wordsworth in Cardiff. I went back . . . and everything had become smaller, and the old sense of awe and greatness had departed. Everything had become simpler and things have been explained.[5]

Have we gained anything? We certainly have, and among our gains I count the gains of our losses. Through the loss of the power of recovery, we have gained the ability to rest. In the ability to rest lies the secret of facing and grasping and mastering the profoundest things of the soul. . . . I can sit quiet now, and hear voices I could not hear amid that din and rush . . . and when a man can be still he comes to know that God is God.[6]

Through the loss of self-confidence we have learned to obey. Through the loss of self-confidence we have learned the secret of sitting at the gate of the King waiting His command. Through the loss of the power of resistance we have learned the ability to take refuge. . . . We dare not put ourselves into places of peril save only as all the times we feel the Presence of the Divine Hand, and know the nearness of One who is mightier than we.[7]

Through the loss of wonder we have gained the power of worship. . . . In the proportion as with the passing years we cease to wonder at the things which come and go, our wonder in the Presence of God who is changing develops and increases.[8]

What we ask of life is that we may be set free from certain forms of service, not for idleness, but that we do so less in order to the doing of more, that we may employ the greater gains that the years have brought us in the increase of our fellow-men; in order that with increasing faith, in order that with more patient hope we may recover hope when it fades in the lives of others; in order that with developed and enlarged love, we may provide a refuge for those who need our help.[9]

I have seen the end of all perfection. It is the old man who is climbing the hill. That is the language of a man who has ascended the hill and is seeing the top, and is seeing clearly the things not done, which were to have been done, but which will never be done . . . but that climbing man is seeing more. He is seeing the broad commandment of God, with the promise of more ultimate spiritual realization; so that while he knows hope deferred, which has made him sick at heart, he now has a new hope in God, which presently will be lost in sight, when faith in full fruition dies.[10]

As I get older my sympathies get far broader in many directions, and I thank God for all I find of the true spirit of Christ in many places where I never looked for it in olden days.[11]

Morgan at age 50

The very comfort as the years run on and the old resilience of youth is no more, or at least is less, of beginning to understand the real significance of the word we have so often used in our heyday, "My grace is sufficient."[12]

Morgan at age 58

Concerning the Advantages of Advancing Age: It was Mark Twain who said that he had done many mean things in his life, but was never mean enough to congratulate a man being fifty years old! Well, in spite of the conception that lies behind, I *am* inclined to congratulate a man who has reached his sixtieth birthday, for after all is said and done, there are enormous advantages round one with these later decades of life. [13]

Morgan at age 71

I learn that, for you, the lease is running out. Well, I beat you to it, for mine ran out on December 9, last year. The fact that the lease runs out does not mean the tenancy ends, for there may be an extension. I hope that, for you, it will be a lengthy one, and one in which you will prove by experience what you have long believed, that at eventide there is light.[14]

Morgan at age 71

I have become very conscious of physical weakness, and indeed the strain of preaching has become too much for me. I have heard the Divine Voice saying, "Ye have tarried long enough on this mount." So I am going, resting assured that the government of God is not only disturbing, but also progressive and methodical.[15]

Morgan at age 80

It is a great thing to find that, even though vigour decreases, the light on the other end of the road abides, and though earthly shadows may be lengthening, one does not feel that one is going down the hill, but up.[16]

Jacob called the name of the place Peniel: for, said he, I have seen God face to face, and my life is preserved.

Genesis 32:30

By this crippling I (Jacob) have come to crowning. By this breaking I have come to making. There in the darkness has come upon me a hand mightier than my own; a force has taken hold of me and broken me, and yet out of it I have come into a new place of power, a new place of life. I have yielded and am crowned. I have been bent and set on high. I have been mastered and have become master. So God brought him to realise his own weakness, and revealed to him the secret of all strength. Forgive the reminiscence. Ten years I was pastor of a church in North London, which is still dear to my heart. Stricken, smitten, and afflicted, I came to the very borderland of eternity; spent a day and a night, expecting to cross over. After I came back to life the first man I went to see was Joseph Parker of the City Temple, who to me was always tender as a mother. I said to him, "I do not understand the experience through which I have passed. I cannot understand this suffering, the sorrow, the breaking of it." He put his hand on my shoulder and said, "My boy, never mind; your people will get the value; there will come another note into your preaching which you could never have found if you had not suffered." I went back, and said, "If this is so, then thank God for all the breaking and all the pain."[17]

8   Facing the End of Life

Of all his ministerial activities, G. Campbell Morgan loved teaching and preaching most. Whether it was a Friday night Bible study in which he would use chalk to sketch out his lesson plan on a huge blackboard behind him or speaking from the pulpit on a Sunday morning in Europe or America, it was helping others appreciate and apply the words of Scripture that he loved. Imagine, then, how he must have felt when as early as 1934 he began to experience a sense of dread when preaching, perhaps brought on by his exhausting schedule, sometimes resulting in attacks of vertigo and a few times even amnesia. He was seventy-one at the time, but these symptoms may have signaled what was to come—a diminishing capacity to do the work he loved.

At seventy-one years old, Morgan began to serve a second time as minister of Westminster Congregational Church, London. His sermons became briefer, rarely exceeding a half hour in length. He tried to cut down on how many times he spoke a week or took on additional evangelistic work. He also began to revisit some of the places that meant so much to him in his lifetime—Tetbury, England, his birthplace; the Wye Valley in Wales where he spent time touring; Market Drayton where he and his wife had married; Monmouth and Cardiff, Wales, where his family had lived; Rugeley, England, a congregation he loved; Birmingham, England, where he had served. It was a chance for him to assess his own life story and gather strength for the final part of his journey. In the summer of 1937, he traveled to the United States once again, spending time with family and speaking in the Tabernacle Presbyterian Church now served by his son, Howard.

In a lecture at Tabernacle, Campbell Morgan grasped what was ahead: "I am conscious that the shadows are lengthening, but now I understand as never before the words, 'Cast thy bread upon the waters; for thou shalt find it after many days.' I am constantly receiving messages that tell me of results from my work in years long ago."[1]

When he was seventy-four, Morgan wrote to a son: "I am thankful that I am able to do what I am doing, and that is two services a week, Friday night, and once on Sunday. I quite honestly feel it is all I am equal to, and whereas the doing of the work is in itself a joy, it produces sometimes an almost terrible sense of exhaustion."[2]

As he neared the end of his life, the tone changed dramatically: "I preached last Sunday morning but I hope I never have a similar experience. My sense of weakness was appalling, and I felt thoroughly unfit for the job."[3] In 1943, two years before he died, Campbell Morgan confessed in a letter just before he announced his resignation from Westminster Church: "Preaching has become a great trial; and although people are good enough to say they know they are still helped, I know personally how different preaching is now to what it was. However not knowing what a day may bring forth, I await the end with quiet confidence."[4]

In 1943, he offered his resignation as Westminster pastor and in August preached to a congregation of some two thousand people on this text from the Gospel of Matthew: "Lo, I am with you." He and his wife, Annie, were now living at St. Ermin's, a hotel within two blocks of the church. He would write from here, "I have become very conscious of physical weakness, and indeed the strain of preaching has become too much for me. I have heard the Divine Voice saying,

'Ye have tarried long enough on this mount.' So I am going, resting assured that the government of God is not only disturbing, but also progressive and methodical."[5]

Dr. Morgan had written a letter when he was seventy-five about the journey he knew was ahead of him: "It often seems strange to look back across the years and remember the experiences of the past. I don't think I desire to go back anywhere. Perhaps the only reason for such a feeling is that, at times, one finds restriction irksome . . . at the same time it is inevitable, and necessary, and wholly beneficial. It is a great thing to find that, even though vigor decreases, the light on the road abides, and though early shadows may be lengthening, one does not feel one is going down the hill, but rather up."[6]

G. Campbell Morgan died May 16, 1945. He was eighty-two years old. At his memorial service at Westminster Church, Dr. D. Martyn Lloyd-Jones, his successor there, recalled visiting him at St. Ermin's the day he died and told those gathered at the service, "That intelligence of his persisted until almost the last moment of his life. . . . It was somewhere round about half past twelve, and he was obviously dying. I tried to be natural, and to speak as I always spoke to him, and I left with the impression that I had not revealed in any way my feeling that that was to be our last meeting on earth.

"However, a short time afterward, he was visited by his doctor, and he said to her, 'I am dying.' 'What makes you think that?' she asked. 'I saw it in Lloyd-Jones's face.' He was dying; life was ebbing away; but with that flashing eye and that keen intelligence of his he was watching me; and he diagnosed my feeling aright."[7]

Campbell Morgan might well have said what he once wrote to another in a letter: "At eventide there is light."[8]

The following excerpts are from the sermon, "The Vanquished Enemy," preached by G. Campbell Morgan on May 30, 1913, at Westminster Congregational Church, London, England. It was a sermon that arose out of the loss of a young man who was seriously thinking about going into the ministry.

The last enemy that shall be abolished is death.

1 Corinthians 15:26

Death is not robed in garments of beauty. It is named an enemy. Its long persistent power is recognized. It is the *last* enemy to be abolished. . . .

Nevertheless the exclamation occurs in the midst of great words, vibrant with victory. "He must reign till He hath put all His enemies under His feet."

Death to humanity is always hostile and hateful. Of all the forces natural and spiritual, death is the least under human control. Life is far more under human control than death. Death continues age after age, century after century, defying every attempt that man has made to discover its secret and to abolish it. We grant the benefits and the blessings that are ours in this age of scientific investigation and progress; but science has done nothing to deal with death. It has done much to alleviate pain, but not to deal with death. . . . Paul's word *echthros*, hateful, hostile, an enemy, is humanity's word, and Christianity has not attempted to change it. . . .

Thus death persists, and man's hatred of it is part of his underlying and undestroyed relationship to the eternities. The protest of man against death is holy, for death remains an enemy. If it be objected that this is hardly the usual language of Christianity about death, I again remind you that this is the language of the apostolic exclamation in the midst of his argument for resurrection; and as the years pass on

I have a growing sense of the hostility and hatefulness of death. . . .

Nevertheless . . . there are limits; sooner or later death comes. What then is to be the Christian attitude towards its victory? It must be that of confidence. We must resolutely refuse to allow the physical in death to be the supreme thing in our consciousness. There must be in the presence of death the determined contemplation of all that is unseen to mortal eyes. We must always remind ourselves when we stand in the presence of our dead ones that the appearance upon which our eyes of sense are fixed is not all the fact. Just beyond the possibility of our human observation are realities definite and eternal. . . . I stand by the side of my dead comrade. There he lies. Oh, but if I am a Christian man I must ever look through and beyond, and say to myself by the side of his coffin, which the angel said of old in Joseph's garden. He is not here, he also is risen. . . .

When in March I went down to my friend, I sat and talked with this lad; he had begun to preach in the villages. I said to him . . . I hope to see you at Cheshunt some day [the Congregational seminary in Cambridge]. The boy did not answer me. He looked at me and I saw the light of wonder and hope in his eyes. And now I am inclined to say, it is all over! It is not all over! My judgment was inaccurate. I thought he might serve in a higher sphere than that in which he was occupied. But God has said to him that He needed him for a still higher sphere than I thought of.

Oh death, I hate thee, but thou art not master of the situation! Jesus is King. The risen Lord and Master reigns. . . . While we yet share in His sufferings in our losses, we will dare to rejoice in His gains, for in the ultimate, final economy, by every soul that passes over, God gains and the day of the last victory is hastened.

What, then, is the Christian teaching? First, that Christ has abolished death. . . . But it might be said, Is not the Cross of Christ the central fact of Christianity? In some senses, yes; but let me remind you . . . that apart from the resurrection the Cross of Christ is nothing other than a tragedy. . . . The cross is vulgar, brutal, devilish; until, seeing it transfigured by the glory of the risen Christ, I am driven back to gaze once more upon that awful mystery, and to discover, shining out of the heart of the unfathomable darkness, the light that never was on land or sea, in which men may walk even though they have sinned, and in the walking find themselves cleansed and made . . . for the dwelling of the saints in light.

The resurrection is the central fact. . . . Yet how often have I heard this said by Christian men and women . . . : Oh, if we might be sure, but no one has come back to tell us. But . . . surely we forget that the central fact of Christianity is that Someone did come back from death to tell us of life; and in that coming back, having died and risen from the dead, He abolished death.

What is the true Christian spirit in the presence of the fact of death?

The first fact . . . is that the true attitude of the Christian toward death is that of antagonism, conflict. . . . The Christian . . . must ever be in conflict with death by every method. By the observation of the laws of health, and the employment of all medical science and skill, death is to be held away. . . .

Those who are gone are with Christ. Those who are left have Christ with them. This is the true communion of saints. We have not lost our loved ones. . . . They are ours and we are theirs. God has them in His keeping till the morning without clouds shall break, and we shall meet to part no more in the land all sunlit, whence the night shades flee.[9]

In all thy ways acknowledge him, and he will direct thy paths.

Proverbs 3:6

This text has a peculiar place in my heart. It has been with me day by day for three and thirty years. It was on the morning when I was first leaving home for school that my father said to me as his last word, "I want to give you a text for school and for life." And it was the text [Proverbs 3:6]. He gave it to me without note or comment, save the note and comment of his own godly life.

In order that we may understand the message of the text, let us first consider one or two simple facts. Within the consciousness of man there exists a dual sense: that of possibility and that of limitation. . . . Every man is conscious of limitation. . . . Every youth and every maiden, in that golden age when the light is forever flashing upon the Eastern shore, comes to this twofold consciousness. In youth this dual consciousness causes perpetual delight. . . . In old age, . . . the limitation becomes everything.

I am yesterday by the side of an old man whose years have reached fourscore and ten, and he said two things to me which profoundly impressed me. He said first: As I lie here and think and listen, that of the world which most profoundly impresses me is its sin. Then, with a light in his eye, he said: "I want to be away, to be with Christ in God."

I feel as though I would like to stay and preach to that old man for a moment. You tell me, looking back, that you dreamed your dreams, and built your castles in the air, and have failed. I ask you: How do you know that you have failed? If according to your light, and in the measure of the opportunity which has come to you, you have been true to God, then just beyond the limit where the infinite sky kisses

107

the finite earth, you will discover that the commonplaces of your life are transfigured into part of God's great whole of perfect work.

The final test of life is beyond the things of time and sense. It will be a test of fire; only that which cannot be destroyed will remain. In the light of that final test . . . we must begin right. What is the first step? Surrender. What is the plan of life, pathway to the end? Obedience.[10]

Men fear death because the beyond is unfamiliar; but the beyond is not unfamiliar to us. We know the country well to which the loved ones go. But you say, that is the difficulty, we do not. Think again. I am afraid the Church of God is losing that great and gracious art of contemplating the country beyond. . . .

Christ does not rebuke your tears. The boy you have let go far away across the ocean, you miss him yet, but he is not as safe as the child Jesus took to be with Himself.[11]

The resurrection of Christ is the pledge of our own resurrection. We are all sorrowing for loved ones gone. Time is a great healer, but it never quite heals. Time never fills the gap. If time were all that had come to heal my heart for the loss of my child it would not be healed even today. Two and a half years old she was when the Master took her. Time has not completely healed the wound, but I have been glad all through the years because of the fact that He rose, and the consequent assurance that I have that so shall she. Not as a child shall I again behold her, but a fair maiden in her Father's mansion. But I shall see her. Unbelief comes to me and says: How do you know? No one has ever come back. The Man, Jesus, came back; and they saw Him, and ate with Him. Here is the proof of the survival of personality after death. The proof is the living Christ. Over the grave of my darling, and over the graves of all our loved ones, there shines the sweet light of His resurrection. We sorrow, oh yes! But we sorrow not as those that have no hope, for we know that in Jesus will God bring them with Him.[12]

Conclusion

Transformed by Grace

Throughout his long life and ministry, G. Campbell Morgan experienced many personal and national crises. They brought moments of doubt and despair which, for him, made him wonder whether God's presence fell more on the side of a question mark than an exclamation point.

Yet always, Morgan clung to hope. Despite personal difficulties, major health problems, the end of his dreams for Westminster Chapel, and national crises, Morgan kept the faith and faced the future with hope. Morgan had said, "Tears are there, but the rain of our tears in the light of the resurrection creates the rainbow which arches all the sky and is the perpetual witness to the ultimate victory."[1] Near the end of his ministry, in a sermon, "But One Thing," Morgan commented on how Portugal changed words on a coin after Columbus discovered America. No longer did the inscription say, "Ne Plus Ultra" (Nothing More Beyond), but "Plus Ultra" (More Beyond). He said, "As we approach the limit, we find light from beyond breaking in on us. We see lying on the other side of what we thought of as consummation and completion, vistas and things unknown and undiscovered . . . to say out through the pillars, 'More beyond.'"[2] That was a keynote in his preaching: always more beyond.

His final four sermons, *Alpha the Last,*[3] were preached at Westminster Chapel in August of 1943 and later published in a little monograph.

Each sermon seemed to accentuate a positive note of hope that whatever life brought, God's presence could transform even the worst events into moments of grace. His last four sermons were as follows:

August 1, 1943—The Government of Human Life

August 8, 1943—Underneath are the Everlasting Arms

August 22, 1943—My Times in Thy Hands

August 29, 1943—The Ever-Present Christ

Kathleen Morgan, Campbell Morgan's daughter, was present at the last service and said, "It was a most inspiring service in every way. . . . There was to be no sadness of farewell, but the onward look. It was the last time I saw him stand in the pulpit, and it was like a most beautiful benediction from start to finish. He preached on the text from the last words of Matthew, 'Lo, I am with you . . .' It was not a long sermon, certainly not as full as I have often heard him preach on that text, but it said all that was needed and the emphasis was not the point that though Dad was laying down his ministry at Westminster, God was not leaving Westminster."[4]

After his final sermon, Campbell Morgan left the pulpit, never to return. The strong voice that had brought courage and strength to thousands was now silenced. In a matter of months, Morgan joined the Church Triumphant, as echoes of his last words might be heard from the towers of Westminster Chapel.

God, the same abiding,
His praise shall tune my voice,
For while in Him confiding,
I cannot but rejoice.[5]

The following are excerpts from four of Campbell Morgan's final sermons.

Jehovah our God spake unto us in Horeb, saying, Ye have dwelt long enough in this mountain.

Deuteronomy 1:6

I arrive nowhere but that God has been ahead of me . . . there is some man, some woman, some youth or some maiden, buffeted, broken, perplexed, lonely, almost mad with the agony of life . . . God was ahead of you. Out of the terror of the hour He is creating forces of triumph in your life which would always have been missing, had you not pitched your tent right there where He has appointed the place.[6]

Campbell Morgan is known today for his biblical preaching and teaching. What is often missed is the strong pastoral note in his preaching. Except for the years when he was itinerating in the States, he was a pastor. He served nine pastorates in his lifetime, even serving twice at Westminster Chapel. Out of his own life experiences he knew how to resonate with those who sat in the pews. He was never the pedantic, scholarly preacher who gave his sermons and disappeared. He was the preacher-pastor all his life.

To be governed by God is to be constantly disturbed, to have human arrangements interfered with. Here is a man whom God has called to some definite piece of work, and in the place of service, he is conscious of the Divine presence, the Divine blessing. It may be that after a period of toil and travail everything is coming into adjustment and the golden radiance of harvest is on the field. Then suddenly to the soul of the man comes the voice of God. "Ye have dwelt long enough in this mountain." The work must be left, the location changed, and all the experience of the past apparently contradicted. The man is disturbed, and that by the Divine government.[7]

"Ye have dwelt long enough in this mountain"; leave that sphere of work which you love so well, be severed from that comrade without whom you feel you cannot live; know the break-up of home. What is God doing with you? Developing the powers of your own life, enabling you to discover the things in you which are of Himself, bearing you on His pinions in the moment of utterest weakness, until presently He teaches you to use your wings He has given you. A disturbing element, but a progressive element.[8]

Fears of suffering, its reason and value, not so much our suffering as that of others. Weakness, physical, spiritual and moral. Is there any agony more poignant than physical weakness, when we become so weak physically that we can lift no finger? And death.

We have seen it, we have observed it, and admittedly, accordingly to biblical teaching, it is the last enemy. . . . Nothing in the mystery of life, strange mystery, is unknown to Him: and there is nothing with which He cannot deal. Underneath all suffering He encircles our sorrows with His own; but in that there is not despair, no weakness . . . in the last reach in the descent, we find His arms.[9]

The eternal God is thy dwelling-place, And underneath are
the everlasting arms.

Deuteronomy 33:27

There are two realms of mystery which persistently assault
the soul of man, and produce within it, the sense of fear.
They are those of the unknown future and the unfathomed
present.[10]

Whatever the abyss, however it seems to be a darkling void,
dare it, dive into it deeply enough, and we reach the cradle of
the arms of God, Underneath! We cannot get beneath that.
It touches the lowest depths of which imagination is capable:
"Underneath are the everlasting arms."[11]

Let us consult our fears. . . . We have fears for the future of
the world in the midst of chaos and apparent hopelessness of
conditions; fears for the Church of God oftentimes as we think
of its confusion and comparative powerlessness at such a time
as this. . . . Then to come to the personal fears, fears of my own
soul, conscious of my weakness by reason of my experience,
conscious of my oft-times failure, I become afraid.

Now the answer to all that fear is this. The God of the
beginning is thy dwelling place. . . . Underneath are the everlasting arms. Nothing in the mystery of life . . . is unknown
to Him; and there is nothing with which He cannot deal.
Underneath all suffering He encircles our sorrows with His
own . . . that God who is our dwelling-place, the God of the
beginning is the God of the everlasting arms. It is impossible
to sink beneath them. They are always underneath.[12]

In a letter from Campbell Morgan's youngest son, Dr. Howard Moody
Morgan, we find this pastoral note in his preaching:

He always looked his congregation in the eye . . . indeed I was present in a church when he rose to preach, the lights in the main sanctuary were dimmed. But Dr. Campbell Morgan stopped his sermon to say, "Will the ushers be so good as to turn on those lights again? I have to see the faces of my congregation; indeed, they are generally a part of my notes."[13]

Lo, I am with you always, even unto the end of the world.

Matthew 28:20

Or "Lo, I am with you all the days, even unto the consummation of the age."

This is the third time over a period of about twenty-five years that I have spoken from this text from this pulpit. I closed the first period of my ministry at Westminster in the year 1917, and again on January 28th I took this text. I took it again at the completion of my visit in 1932, on September 25th. I made no apology for repeating myself. What I say about the text will be about what I said before, and what I say about the text never matters. It is the text that matters. . . . While the words are thus for all the days, they make special appeal to such of those who are facing critical days. Whenever His own stand at the parting of the ways, the music of them brings courage and inspiration to the soul.[14]

And this is the word of perfect patience and power. "I am with you all the days," in places of difficulty in which he may lead us, or the paths of foolishness into which we may wander. . . . I am with you in times of danger, danger through adversity, all the more subtle danger of prosperity; for there are more men and women fall from the faith through prosperity than through adversity. Well, if we fall, if we wander, if we are in danger, He is still with us.[15]

And then finality of the word, "Unto the end of the world," "unto the consummation of the age." . . . When riches are nothing, and when health and strength are gone, when friends, the most loving and tender are quite helpless, when the means of grace fail, the Presence in the gloom is that of this self-same Lord and Master. And may we carry the thought further? He will be with us to the eternal ages. That will be the essence of heaven to be where He is, and to see Him, and to hear Him, and to work with Him, for He is not idle, neither are the saints that have gone, idle. They rest from their labors, but their works, not follow after them, but accompany them forth. They are still working, and we shall be." . . . The changes of life should ever renew our sense of the abiding Christ. The men to whom He spoke the words were those who had heard, obeyed, and followed; and if we hear His voice, and obey, and are following, it is ours too. "Lo, I am with you all the days," dark days, bright days, shadowed days, sunlit days, all the days I am with you.[16]

Here, then, is the answer to our fears. We still admit these mysteries of tomorrow and today, but we find our rest in God. He is the beginning. He is always the beginning of every day, and of every tomorrow; and that God who is our dwelling place, the God of the beginning is the God of the everlasting arms. It is impossible to sink beneath them. They are always underneath.[17]

My times are in thy hand.

Psalm 31:15

In this sermon, it appears that Campbell Morgan is reminiscing about his life and over 60 years of ministry. In a real way, his faith story is a legacy he left to his family and succeeding generations.

Our lives resemble a patchwork quilt. We start with scraps of material passed on to us: our genetic makeup, our family history and tradition. Then we add our own materials. Finally we take all these pieces of material and put them together and they become a unique pattern of our own making. When pieced together the stories become a beautiful quilt.

"My times." Well, what about them? What about past years? Oh, the pain, the failure, the sins, and breakdown; and also we had glad days, days when one lived, lived in the consciousness of communion with God; and all the commonplaces of life become radiant with the glory of the eternal past. They are gone. "My times are in Thy hands." All the past.[18]

Look back over the past, or look at the present. Times of sorrow, times of joy; times of defeat, when I am broken and beaten, times of victory when I rise triumphantly; times of sickness, when one hardly knows how to crawl; times of health when everything becomes a delight; times of need, when one can hardly know any resources to meet necessity; times of abundance, when there be no need to care. Good times, bad times, what about them? They are all in His hand.[19]

As I look into those hands of God there are wound prints; and I know these hands are redeeming hands. Creating hands, but the vessel is marred. Guiding hands, but I have run away. Redeeming hands. He has come to bring me back. . . . "My times are in Thy hands." That is the comfort of the backward look. If any man can look back on the past years with complete satisfaction, he is a shallow, superficial sort of man. There they are in those years, the days of failures, blunders, weaknesses. The supreme truth about them all is this. "My times are in Thy hands." God can deal with them and I leave them with Him.

It is also the courage of the forward look,

> I know not what awaits me,
> God kindly veils my eyes;
>
> And o'er each step of my onward way,
> He makes new scenes to rise.

Sometimes I am frightened, and then I say, "My times are in Thy hands," and I am quiet and strong when I remember.[20]

Oh, this is a very human thing to say. I told you I was going to use human language. It means His untiring love. And this is a word of untiring patience and power. "I am with you all the days," in places of difficulty into which He may lead us, or the paths of foolishness into which we may wander. I remember hearing a man say once if we got into difficulty under Divine guidance, we could look for Divine deliverance and release, but if we got into difficulty through our own folly, we must work our way out. Nonsense! Into any place of difficulty where we may go, it may be reason of our own foolishness, He is with us. "I am with you all the days."[21]

Dr. Morgan carefully and meticulously recorded all of his sermons in beautiful handwriting. The Register (a listing of G. Campbell Morgan's sermons written in his own hand) records 1,639 sermons, written and delivered from 1889 to 1943. His last written sermon was entitled "Two Routes to the King's Palace," and excerpts are included here.

When I am afraid,

I will put my trust in thee.
In God (I will praise his word),

In God have I put my trust, I will not be afraid. . . .
In God have I put my trust, I will not be afraid.

Psalm 56:3–4, 11

I am more inclined to talk with you than to preach to you this morning. I have read this psalm and have taken these words as the subject of meditation because they have been talking to me in a very practical and definite and personal way during these weeks that have passed. It is more than forty years ago now that my attention was first drawn to the texts I have read this morning by a young man who went out from my church in Birmingham to enter the ministry. . . . One day I got a postcard from him, and when I looked at it, this is what I read: There are ways to the crystal Palace, the Low Level and the Level; and David described the Low Level when he said, "At what times I am afraid, I will put my trust in Thee." But he described the High Level when he said, "I will trust and not be afraid." As I have said this is more than forty years ago, I have never forgotten it, and it has been coming back to me in these weeks and months with great force. That is why I read this psalm and take this text. . . .

Can you say, When I am afraid I will trust? Then you are journeying home to God. Only, let it be admitted, let it be said in conclusion that the higher is in this case the better way; it is better to say, I will not be afraid than to ever say when I am afraid I will trust. That is what I am trying to do. There have been moments in these months when I have been afraid, and yet I can honestly say when those moments have come I have said I will trust. It is a great, heroic decision of will.

It is great to do that. But I want to know what it is to travel the higher way, to be able to say as to these dark and sinister days pass on as they go, I will not be afraid; and that ability is created by the consciousness admitted and yielded to, that God is nearer than all our foes, Master of all our circumstances, over-ruling every dispensation of these dark days.

So, let us lift our eyes, whatever coming days may bring us, and we do not know what a day may bring forth; we do know one thing, God; and

> While in Him abiding,
> His praise shall tune my voice;
> For while in Him confiding,
> I cannot but rejoice.[22]

Dr Martyn Lloyd-Jones, who succeeded Campbell Morgan at Westminster Chapel, spoke some definitive words at the memorial service. He said, "He, surely, was the supreme illustration of the fact that God always gives His gifts at the right time. If ever it could be said of a man that he was man for his age, that can be said of Dr. Campbell Morgan. . . . This great evangelistic movement [Moody and Sankey] had come into the whole life of the Church, and what was needed above everything else at that point was someone who could teach these converts. And 'a man came from God whose name was George Campbell Morgan,' and he came at the critical moment, at the very right time."[23]

This may well be another right time for the words of G. Campbell Morgan to speak of grace and hope for our embattled world.

Suggested Readings

Chicago Theological Seminary holds a collection of G. Campbell Morgan's books, periodicals, unpublished manuscripts, and other materials. If interested, contact Mr. Howard C. Morgan at Chicago Theological Seminary, 5727 S. University Ave., Chicago, Illinois 60637.

Primary Sources

Note: Only a selected number of Campbell Morgan's eighty books are listed that are pertinent to this book. The full collection is kept in the Chicago Theological Seminary Library.

Books

Crises of the Christ. New York: Fleming H. Revell, 1903.
Discipleship. New York: Fleming H. Revell, 1897.
An Exposition of the Whole Bible. New York: Fleming H. Revell, 1959.
First Century Message to Twentieth Century Christians. Grand Rapids: Baker Books, 1980.

The Great Physician. London: Marshall, Morgan, and Scott, 1937.

The Ministry of the Word. New York: Fleming H. Revell, 1919.

Treasury of G. Campbell Morgan. Grand Rapids: Baker Books, 1972.

The Westminster Pulpit. 5 Vol. Grand Rapids: Baker Books, 2006.

Periodicals, Booklets, and Pamphlets

"How to Read the Bible." Northfield Conference, 1901, 6.

Alpha and Omega. Coventry, England: Curtis and Beamish, Ltd., Printers, 1943, 56.

Correspondence

Letters from G. Campbell Morgan to his son, F. Crossley Morgan.

Letters in Jill Morgan's book, *This Was His Faith*.

Secondary Sources

Books

Fant, Clyde Jr. and William M. Pinson Jr. *20 Centuries of Great Preaching: An Encyclopedia of Preaching*, Vol. 81. From Morgan to Coffin, Waco, Texas: Word, 1983.

Harries, John. *G. Campbell Morgan: The Man and His Ministry*. New York: Fleming H. Revell, 1930.

Jeffs, Earnest M. *Princes of the Modern Pulpit in England*. Nashville: Cokesbury, 1931.

McCartney, Clarence Edward. *Great Sermons of the World*. Boston: The Stratford Company, 1926.

Morgan, Jill. *A Man of the Word: Life of G. Campbell Morgan*. New York: Fleming H. Revell, 1952.

———*This Was His Faith: The Expository Letters of G. Campbell Morgan*. New York: Fleming H. Revell, 1952.

Morrison, Charles Clayton, ed. *The American Pulpit*. New York: Macmillan, 1925. Based on a Christian Century survey of 2,000 preachers.

Murray, Harold. *Campbell Morgan: Bible Teacher*. London: Marshall, Morgan and Scott, 1938.

Wagner, Don M. *The Expository Method of G. Campbell Morgan*. Westwood, NJ: Fleming H. Revell, 1957.

Periodical Articles

Bishop, John. "G. Campbell Morgan, Man of the Word." *Preaching*. (March–April, 1991): 59–60.

Chadwick, Samuel M. "Dr. Campbell Morgan's Ten Years at Westminster." *Westminster Bible Record*. (1914): 82.

Dudit, Michael. "Ten Greatest Preachers of the 20th Century." *Preaching* XV, no. 3. (November–December, 1999).

Kaye, Elaine. "G. Campbell Morgan." *Dictionary of National Biography*, vol. 39.

Unpublished Dissertation

Baggett, Hudson. "The Principles and Art of G. Campbell Morgan as a Bible Expositor." PhD dissertation, Southern Baptist Seminary, 1956, 253.

Katt, Arthur Frederick. "A Rhetorical Analysis of the Preaching of G. Campbell Morgan." Indiana University, June, 1963, 301 (Available from UMI Dissertation Services, Box 1346, Ann Arbor, Michigan, 48106-1346.)

Internet

www.gospelcom.net, link: sermon index
www.ChurchinWestland.org
www.brooksidebaptist.org/book_reviews_morgan
www.christianbook.com/

Notes

Foreword

1. Personal communication, June 27, 2006.
2. 2003, Phyllis Pennese; 2004, Elaine (Harriet) Joyner-Sander; 2005, Jerry Hancock; 2006, Anthony Hollins.
3. Toni Morrison, *Paradise* (New York: Alfred A. Knopf, 1997), 273.

Introduction

1. *Preaching*, November–December 1999, 10.
2. G. Campbell Morgan, "Jacobs's Lameness," *Westminster Record*, September 4, 1909.
3. G. Campbell Morgan, "The Crippling That Crowns," *Westminster Pulpit*, vol. 7, 348.
4. G. Campbell Morgan, "Secret and Revealed Things," *Westminster Pulpit*, vol. 3, January 31, 1908.
5. G. Campbell Morgan, letter to son, dated July 2, 1941.
6. Ibid.
7. G. Campbell Morgan, "Nineteen Minutes of Reminiscences," *Westminster Record*, 1936.
8. Jill Morgan, *A Man of the Word* (Grand Rapids: Baker, 1972), 398.

Chapter 1: Eclipse of Faith and Transformation of Life

1. Jill Morgan, ed., *This Was His Faith* (Englewood Cliffs, NJ: Revell, 1952), 38–40.
2. G. Campbell Morgan, "Christ and Thomas," *Westminster Pulpit*, vol. 3, December 24, 1908, 414.

3. G. Campbell Morgan, "Was Thomas Mistaken?" *Westminster Pulpit*, vol. 5, April 22, 1916, 131.

4. Campbell Morgan, "Christ and Thomas," 411.

5. Ibid., 415.

6. G. Campbell Morgan, "Jubilation in Desolation," *Westminster Pulpit*, vol. 6, July 1911, 222.

7. Campbell Morgan, "Christ and Thomas," 416

8. G. Campbell Morgan, "Burning of the Heart," *Westminster Pulpit*, vol. 11, April 20, 1906, 1.

9. Ibid., 7.

10. Ibid., 12.

11. Ibid., 8.

12. G. Campbell Morgan, "The Misuse of Scripture," *Westminster Pulpit*, vol. 1, October 19, 1906, 1.

13. Ibid., 6.

14. Ibid., 4.

15. Ibid., 8.

16. Ibid.

17. G. Campbell Morgan, "How to Read the Bible," *Northfield Reporter*. From an address delivered at Northfield, Massachusetts, 1901.

18. G. Campbell Morgan, "Famine for the Word of God," *Westminster Pulpit*, vol. 2, July 10, 1907, 2.

19. G. Campbell Morgan, "The Bible and National Life," *Westminster Pulpit*, vol. 5, February 18, 1910, 57, 63.

20. Jill Morgan, *This Was His Faith*, 218.

Chapter 2: Rejected on Earth, Accepted in Heaven

1. Jill Morgan, *A Man of the Word*, 60.

2. Ibid.

3. Ibid., 68.

4. Ibid., 69.

5. Ibid., 73.

6. John Harries, *G. Campbell Morgan: The Man and His Ministry* (New York: Fleming H. Revell, 1930), 76.

7. Jill Morgan, *A Man of the Word*, 69.

8. G. Campbell Morgan, "Guidance by Hindrance," unpublished sermon, 1916.

9. G. Campbell Morgan, "Varieties in the Church," *Westminster Record*, August, 1905, 171, 177–78.

10. G. Campbell Morgan, "Workers Together with Christ," sermon preached November 17, 1889, at Stone Congregational Church.

11. Ibid.

12. Ibid.

13. Ibid.

14. Ibid.

15. G. Campbell Morgan, "When God Changes His Plans," undated sermon, Tabernacle Church, Philadelphia.

16. Ibid.

17. Campbell Morgan, "Workers Together."

18. Ibid.

19. Campbell Morgan, "Varieties in the Church," 177.

20. Ibid., 175–76.

21. G. Campbell Morgan, "Underneath the Everlasting Arms," *Alpha and Omega*, Westminster Chapel.

Chapter 3: When Loved Ones Die

1. G. Campbell Morgan, "The Vanquished Enemy," *Westminster Pulpit*, vol. 8, 170–71.

2. Previously unpublished letter, 1934.

3. G. Campbell Morgan, *Christian Principles* (New York: Fleming Revell), 1928, 38–39.

4. G. Campbell Morgan, "Death Abolished," *Westminster Pulpit*, vol. 6, 111–12.

5. Ibid., 103–104.

6. Jill Morgan, *A Man of the Word*, 201.

7. Campbell Morgan, "Death Abolished," 100.

8. Ibid., 105–106.

9. Ibid., 109–10.

10. Ibid., 112.

11. Jill Morgan, *A Man of the Word*, 261–62.

12. Campbell Morgan, "Death Abolished," 259.

13. G. Campbell Morgan, *Searchlights from the Word* (New York: Revell, 1926), 306.

14. Campbell Morgan, "Death Abolished," 112.

15. G. Campbell Morgan, "My Friend," *Westminster Pulpit*, May 11, 1906, 1–3.

16. G. Campbell Morgan, "Albert Swift," *Westminster Pulpit*, January 2, 1914, 1–3.

17. G. Campbell Morgan, "The Christian Outlook Upon Death," *Westminster Pulpit*, March 7, 1914, 5.

18. Campbell Morgan, "The Vanquished Enemy," *Westminster Pulpit*, May 30, 1913, 169, 173–74.

Chapter 4: Confronting Illness

1. G. Campbell Morgan, "Jacob's Lameness," *Westminster Pulpit*, vol. 4, April 16, 1909, 127.

2. Arthur Frederick Katt, *A Rhetorical Analysis of the Preaching of G. Campbell Morgan*, unpublished manuscript, Ann Arbor, MI, 1962, 39. (Letter to Katt from Dr. F. Crossley Morgan, September 11, 1962.)

3. G. Campbell Morgan, "Nineteen Minutes of Reminiscences," *Westminster Record*, 1936, 9–10.

4. Jill Morgan, *A Man of the Word*, 212–13.

5. Address at Northfield Conference, 1901.

6. G. Campbell Morgan, "Five Silent Sundays," *Westminster Pulpit*, 148.

7. Jill Morgan, *A Man of the Word*, 113.

8. Campbell Morgan, "Jacob's Lameness," 127.

9. G. Campbell Morgan, "The Tragedy of Life Without Faith," *Westminster Pulpit*, vol. 9, June 19, 1914.

10. Ibid., 196.

11. Ibid., 199.

12. Ibid., 200.

13. G. Campbell Morgan, "The Healing of Life," *Westminster Pulpit*, vol. 9, March 27, 1914, 103.

14. G. Campbell Morgan, "The Psalm of the Convalescent," *Westminster Bible Record*, February 18, 1915, 76.

15. Ibid., 77.

16. Ibid.

17. Ibid., 78.

18. Ibid., 79.

19. Ibid., 81.

20. G. Campbell Morgan, "Underneath the Everlasting Arms," *Alpha and Omega*, August 22, 1943, 139.

21. G. Campbell Morgan, "My Grace Is Sufficient for Thee," *Westminster Pulpit*, vol. 2, May 31, 1907, 167–68, 172–74.

22. G. Campbell Morgan, "Songs in Prison, *Westminster Pulpit*, vol. 11, July 28, 1916, 235–37.

Chapter 5: When Tragedy Strikes

1. G. Campbell Morgan, *Westminster Record*, vol. 3, May, 1912, 97.

2. Jill Morgan, *This Was His Faith*, 298.

3. G. Campbell Morgan, *God, Humanity, and the War* (London: J. Clark, 1914).

4. John Harries, *G. Campbell Morgan: The Man and His Ministry*, 127–28.

5. Jill Morgan, *A Man of the Word*, 205–206.

6. Ibid., 206.

7. G. Campbell Morgan, "The Wreck of the Titanic," *Westminster Pulpit*, vol. 7, April 26, 1912, 129.

8. Ibid., 130.

9. Ibid.

10. Ibid., 130–31.

11. Ibid.

12. Ibid., 131–32.

13. Ibid.

14. Ibid., 136.

15. G. Campbell Morgan, "The Day of War and the Day of Calamity," *Westminster Pulpit*, vol. 9, August 7, 1914, 249.

16. Ibid., 262.

17. G. Campbell Morgan, "The Life of Faith in the Day of Calamity," *Westminster Pulpit*, vol. 9, August 14, 1914, 262.

18. Ibid., 263.

19. Ibid., 252.

20. G. Campbell Morgan, "War in the Heavenlies," *Westminster Pulpit*, vol. 9, August 21, 1914, 271.

21. Campbell Morgan, *God, Humanity, and the War*, 40.

22. G. Campbell Morgan, "The Valley of Decision," *Westminster Pulpit*, vol. 9, August 28, 1914, 279.

23. Ibid., 282.

24. G. Campbell Morgan, "The Secrets of Peace," *Westminster Pulpit*, vol. 9, September 25, 1914, 305, 312.

25. G. Campbell Morgan, "Of His Kingdom. No End."

26. G. Campbell Morgan, "The Fixed Heart in the Day of Frightfulness," *Westminster Pulpit*, vol. 11, March 3, 1916, 65, 68, 72.

27. G. Campbell Morgan, "The Passing of the King," *Westminster Pulpit*, vol. 5, May, 13, 1910, 155–57.

28. Jill Morgan, *This Was His Faith*, 298.

29. Ibid., 299.

30. Ibid.

Chapter 6: Dreams Deferred

1. G. Campbell Morgan, "Ten Years at Westminster," *Westminster Pulpit*, vol. 40, October 2, 1914, 313–14.

2. Ibid., 314–15.

3. Ibid., 316–18.

4. Ibid.

5. Ibid., 319.

6. Ibid., 319–20.

7. Ibid.

8. G. Campbell Morgan, "Why I Remain at Westminster," vol. 10, July 2, 1915, 209, 211.

9. Ibid., 215.

Chapter 7: Growing Older

1. G. Campbell Morgan, "Fifty Years and After," *Westminster Pulpit*, vol. 8, December 26, 1913, 409.

2. Ibid., 410.

3. Ibid., 411.

4. Ibid.

5. Ibid., 411–12.

6. Ibid., 412.

7. Ibid.

8. Ibid., 413.

9. Ibid., 415.

10. Campbell Morgan, "Ten Years at Westminster," 315.

11. Jill Morgan, *This Was His Faith*, 309.

12. Ibid., 315.

13. Ibid., 314.

14. Ibid., 314–15.

15. Ibid., 319.

16. Ibid., 316.

17. G. Campbell Morgan, "Jacob's Lameness," *Westminster Pulpit*, vol. 4, April 16, 1909, 125, 127.

Chapter 8: Facing the End of Life

1. Jill Morgan, *This Was His Faith*, 299.

2. Letter from G. Campbell Morgan dated December 13, 1937.

3. Letter from G. Campbell Morgan dated March 6, 1941.

4. Letter from G. Campbell Morgan, dated June 19, 1943.

5. Jill Morgan, *This Was His Faith*, 319.

6. Ibid., 317.

7. Jill Morgan, *Man of the Word*, 330.

8. Ibid., 317.

9. G. Campbell Morgan, "The Vanquished Enemy," *Westminster Pulpit*, vol. 8, May 30, 1913, 22.

10. G. Campbell Morgan, "How To Succeed in Life," *Westminster Pulpit*, vol. 4, May 17, 1909, 145, 146, 152.

11. G. Campbell Morgan, "Death Abolished," preached Easter morning, 1910, Westminster Congregational Church, London, England.

12. G. Campbell Morgan, "Our Hope and Inheritance," *Westminster Pulpit*, vol. 10, April 16, 1915, 120.

Conclusion: Transformed by Grace

1. G. Campbell Morgan, "Death Abolished," *Westminster Pulpit*, vol. 8, 112.

2. Ralph Turnbull, ed., "But One Thing," *The Best of G. Campbell Morgan* (Grand Rapids: Baker, 1971), 62.

3. Campbell Morgan, "Alpha the Last," *Alpha and Omega*.

4. Jill Morgan, *Man of the Word*, 316.

5. From the hymn "Joy and Peace in Believing" by William Cowper.

6. Campbell Morgan, "The Government of Human Life," *Alpha and Omega*.

7. Ibid., 28.

8. Ibid., 33.

9. G. Campbell Morgan, "Underneath the Everlasting Arms," *Alpha and Omega*.

10. Ibid., 38.

11. Ibid., 39.

12. Ibid., 38–40.

13. Letter from Dr. Howard Moody Morgan, October 23, 1959, published in Arthur Katt, *A Rhetorical Analysis of the Preaching of G. Campbell Morgan*, 189.

14. Ibid., 55.

15. Ibid., 56.

16. Ibid., 57.

17. G. Campbell Morgan, "Our Times Are in His Hands," *Alpha and Omega*, 45.

18. Ibid.

19. Ibid., 47.

20. Ibid., 57.

21. G. Campbell Morgan, "Two Routes to the King's Palace," *Westminster Record*, vol. 15, May 15, 1941, 53, 57.

22. The Sermon Register, housed in G. Campbell Morgan Memorial Library.

23. "Remarks by Dr. Martyn Lloyd-Jones," *Westminster Record*, July, 1945, 61.

List of Biblical Texts

The following biblical texts or stories are cited in the sermons used in this book. Ordinarily, the translation is from the American Standard Edition (1901) which Morgan preferred. Morgan's selection of biblical texts or stories again illustrates how he related biblical texts to personal or national crises.

Genesis 32:20 99
Numbers 8:25–26 95
Deuteronomy 1:6 113
Deuteronomy 33:27
   60, 115
2 Samuel 7:25 89
Psalm 8:4 73
Psalm 27:13 56
Psalm 29:11 71
Psalm 31:15 117
Psalm 56:3–4 120
Psalm 97:1–2 72

Psalm 112:7 76
Psalm 119:96 83
Proverbs 3:6 107
Isaiah 38:16 58
Amos 8:11 28
Joel 3:14 74

Matthew 28:20 116
Luke 1:33 75
Luke 13:1–3 68
Luke 24:32 26
John 5:39 27

John 14:27 75
John 20:25 24
Acts 16:25–26 62
1 Corinthians 4:16 94
1 Corinthians 15:26
   104
2 Corinthians 6:1 36
2 Corinthians 12:9 60
Ephesians 6:12 72
2 Timothy 1:10 46
1 Peter 1:25 29

List of Sermon Titles

Albert Swift
Bible and National Life
Burning of the Heart
But One Thing
Christ and Thomas
Christian Outlook on Death
Christian Principles
Crippling That Crowns
Day of War and Day of Calamity
Death Abolished
Ever Present Christ
Famine for Hearing the Word of God
Fifty Years and After
Fixed Heart in the Day of
    Frightfulness
Government of Human Life
Guidance by Hindrance
Healing of Life
How to Succeed in Life
Jacob's Lameness
Jubilation in Desolation
Life of Faith in the Day of Calamity

Misuse of Scripture
My Friend
My Grace Is Sufficient for Thee
My Times Are in His Hands
Our Hope and Inheritance
Passing of the King
Secret and Revealed Things
Secrets of Peace
Songs in Prison
Ten Years at Westminster
Tragedy of Life without Faith
Two Routes to the King's Palace
Underneath Are the Everlasting Arms
Valley of Decision
Vanquished Enemy
Varieties in Church's Life
War in the Heavenlies
Was Thomas Mistaken?
When God Changes His Plans
Why I Remain at Westminster
Workers Together with Christ
Wreck of the Titanic

Richard Morgan is an ordained Presbyterian minister and a national leader in spiritual autobiography and issues of aging. He is the author of several books in the field of aging and spirituality, his most recent being *Remembering Your Story, Fire in the Soul,* and *Settling In: My First Year in a Retirement Community.*

Howard Morgan is currently the chairman of Chicago Theological Seminary, a trustee of Court Theatre of Chicago, and a life director of Lincoln Park Zoo and Executive Service Corps. He served as senior vice president of Citibank for 41 years and as director for The American Bible Society and St Ignatius College Preparatory School.

John Morgan, a newspaper columnist and a former pastor and now a Quaker, teaches ethics and philosophy at a community college. His most recent books include *Daybreak and Eventide: A Little Book of Prayer and Worship for Small Groups* and *Awakening the Soul.*